SABRINA FISHER REECE

Mind Is All

Manipulating Ideas In A New Direction

In59Seconds Publishing Co

Contents

One

Mind Is All There Is

~~~~~~~

The one significant thing we were never taught in school was that our mind controls our lives. Yes, your MIND. What does that even mean? Aren't the mind and the brain the same thing?

The brain and the mind differ greatly. The mind is not tangible matter. There is no mind to cut open and dissect. The brain, however, is tangible, and has been explored by scientists for many many years. Yet so many people still question which one is most important.

All of our senses are directly connected to the brain. When you are in physical pain, it is your nervous system that receives and delivers that information to the brain. Your brain is divided into the right and left hemispheres, as well as the frontal, temporal, parietal, and occipital lobes. Each lobe of the brain was designed for its own specific purpose. The brain is so vital, there is more focus on it than the mind. You can not dissect the mind of a human being as you can the brain. You can not physically cut open one's mind and study it, but in my opinion the true essence of who we are is because of this intangible mind. We can't see it, but we all have a mind; a voice inside of us that speaks to and guides us. It's how God communicates to us. Many believe it is the origin of our soul. The mind is what makes

1

each and every one of us individuals. For the most part, human brains are all constructed the exact same way. Each mind, however, vastly differs from the other. Just like fingerprints no one's mind is the same.

Our mind houses our individual thoughts. Through the use of our mind we make choices on how we react to life's experiences. When someone makes us angry, the decision is made in our mind to react in an angry manner. There is no objective display that appears before us and says, "It's time to be mad." We make those choices internally via our minds. The same goes for love and kindness. When the emotion of another suddenly strikes you and you decide to be generous and buy a homeless person a meal or give a young striving person a one-hundred dollar bill, the decision to do so happens inside of you. The action is overt, but the choice to do so isn't. It appears that all of the true significant battles all begin in the mind. We decide if something is logical or reasonable in our minds first before we outwardly react. The mind governs all of our actions. The negotiations begin within. In the case of people who appear to be primarily reactive and impulsive, I do not believe they take those few moments to consult their mind first. They simply react, and that impulsive reaction may not have always been the correct choice. Anger and happiness are both choices that begin in the mind. We can control our minds, as opposed to allowing them to control us.

Do you want to be happy? Happiness begins in the mind. The journey to personal development and living our best lives begins inside. Mind is all. Everything begins there. It is the key to perfect health and abundant wealth and everything else we desire. Learning to properly manipulate our minds is the true key to happiness. Yes we can change our minds. Our thoughts are the missing piece to this creative puzzle. We think thousands of thoughts daily, so many we could not even begin to count them. Counting them is not important but monitoring them is. Teaching ourselves to switch negative thoughts into positive ones is crucial. Learning to maintain a positive thinking pattern is the first step to experiencing the best that life has to offer. All human beings can have a wonderful life.

Having a great life is possible if you accept responsibility for your mind. Like a child, we should never allow our minds to run around unattended.

Children need our parental guidance to grow and develop. The mind is the same. It is just like our child we have to mold and shape. We must guide our mind in the direction of greatness so that we can experience life abundantly. If we do not direct our mind it will direct us. We must steer that ship in our favor. If we do not, tumultuous seas are ahead. We do not have to accept whatever life brings to us. We can use our amazing beautiful minds to carefully direct our thoughts to ensure that we live up to our fullest capabilities and enjoy the world while doing so.

Two

Limitations Are ILLusions

❧

The Mind is not limited. With our minds we can imagine anything we desire. Most people believe the big "secret" of success and happiness is detailed and complicated. I believe the true secret is simple: *We control our lives with our thoughts and imagination.* Through proper use of the imagination, we can bring forth in our lives anything we desire. This is "The Secret." While humans spend billions of dollars and hours of priceless time searching for the secret to mankind, I sincerely believe it's as simple as controlling our reality through our thoughts. Good thoughts produce a good life and bad thoughts produce a bad life. You may not be able to see the Mind but learning to use this invisible power is very important.

I have studied many different religions, ancient philosophers, and various schools of thought. One conclusion I have found is, many of the people that came long before us knew the importance of focusing our thoughts. Somehow, this information got lost. The more I study great people from the past. I realize this knowledge was known and practiced by many. Long before "thinking positive" became a popular fad, it was a known practice of the ancestors.

Thinking positive on purpose can reshape our lives in a favorable direction. Creating internal visual images of our desires in our minds first allows them to become a reality. Neville Goddard says "Our Imagination is God," working with us and through us, allowing us to be a co-creator of our own lives. I am in agreement with Neville on this subject. Our imagination is the tool we can use to bring our desires into reality.

It is through our intentional focused thought and creating a mental image that all things come into existence. You can call this focused thought prayer, imagination, meditation, stillness or mindfulness. It does not matter how you choose to describe it, as long as you come to realize that your thoughts design your life. Yes! This is very important information. The thoughts in your mind create the reality in your tangible life. For those who sincerely believe that life "just happens," I understand why this would be a difficult concept to grasp, but it is true. It may not seem logical to some, but it is definitely the powerful energy that miracles are made of. The legendary Albert Einstein knew the importance of using our minds to imagine when he said, "Logic will get you from A to Z but imagination will get you everywhere". He went on to stress to the world that "Imagination is more important than knowledge. Knowledge is limited. Imagination encircles the world." I elaborate more on the proper use of imagination in chapter 4.

Our minds will attempt to imagine an equal number of negative things. We must control what we imagine. If we allow persistent negative thoughts to occupy space in our minds, we will continue to experience negative situations in our lives. Once we learn to change those negative thoughts to positive thoughts, we will see our lives take a significant turn for the better.

Take control of your thoughts and drive them down the road you want your life to go down. If you do this, you will have a better life experience. Anything you can imagine will become a reality. This is a power given to us by God. Use this power to create a better life. We do not have to settle for a mediocre existence,s we can all experience the best life has to offer. This is not an exclusive pleasure. The great pleasures of this earth are not saved for a limited few. With proper use of the mind, everyone can live a prosperous,

5

fulfilling life. Wealth, great health, success and happiness are here for us all. Every human being can experience the wonderful pleasures of life.

So, how do we control our thoughts? This seems especially difficult since we seem to have thousands of them every minute. How could one ever control them? The simplest answer is by being still long enough to monitor them. Sit still even for five minutes a day. Only then will you be able to identify the negative thoughts. Push those thoughts right out of your head and replace them with more positive thoughts.

I understand this is easier said than done, but I assure you with daily practice it can become a habit. Most of us are well into our thirties and or forties before we begin to realize our thoughts make a difference in our lives. Be patient but consistent with the process. Begin by simply writing down the clear and obvious negative thoughts you recognize. Once you identify them. Start working on each one individually. Sometimes, if you take a moment to think about each one you can find the root of where this negative idea began. For example, if someone in your family died of a particular disease and you remember hearing about and fearing this disease as a child. This is the root of how you formed negative thoughts and fears about this specific illness. It does not have to happen to you. Getting this disease is not an unavoidable certainty. You can reprogram your mind regarding the fear associated with contracting and dying from that disease or any disease for that matter.

As we travel throughout life, we form many beliefs that do not promote a great life. Let's say when you were five years old, your parents had a friend who died in a plane crash. This incident was very traumatic for your parents. You watched them grieve and cry. You even attended the funeral with them. Being too young to fully comprehend the death, all you saw was pain and sadness associated with airplanes. This is precisely where the negative seed was planted and this sparked your fear of flying. These subconscious fears can lay dormant within us for years until something triggers them. It takes intentional, focused quiet time to recognize these triggers and itemize their individual root causes. Although there are incidents throughout our lives that cause us to have certain fears, we do not have to continue to live with them and allow them to affect our lives. We can identify them and change them. You cannot change or reprogram any negative thinking patterns until you realize they exist. The ability to recognize them is a gift. Spend time with your mind. Take a moment to understand which thoughts need to be reversed. Make it your mission to begin the reversal process.

The mind is everything. Without the proper use of the mind, we leave our lives subject to chance. If we are unaware that we have the ability to choose our thoughts, then we will allow all thoughts to run rampant in our mind. We tend to underestimate the magnitude of damage negative thoughts can have. Continuing to allow negative thoughts to take up space in our mind is detrimental to the quality of life we live. Imagine happiness. Imagine wealth. Imagine perfect health. Each one of these is possible for everyone. Take a mere five minutes a day to close your eyes and imagine the life you desire. Begin to feel the visual as reality and soon it will be.

The truth is, **your mind is magic**, and you possess the magic wand. You are in control. You can guide your mind in any direction you choose. That is the wonderful secret that seems to have gotten lost as time progressed. However, many of our ancestors were privy to this power. This amazing gift is extremely powerful, so we must realize what a huge responsibility God has given us.

The mind is a non-judgmental garden. If you plant seeds of negativity and doubt that is exactly what will grow. On the other hand if you plant positive seeds, seeds of greatness, seeds of love, seeds of kindness then your garden will produce just that. So, it's truly all in your hands. This magic I speak of is non-bias. It won't tell you, "No, I refuse to produce this because it's not going to enhance your life." If you plant it, it will grow.

That analogy alone was enough for me to aggressively begin working on my M.I.N.D. techniques. I developed this acronym to help me remember the importance of the mind and maintaining a positive mental attitude.

MIND
M - Manipulating
I - Ideas in a
N - New

D - Direction

Learning to manipulate our ideas in a new direction was the main goal in writing this book. Yes! This helped me to control my mind's magic. If I was attending an event and I walked into the room feeling insecure because of recent weight gain, or maybe my skin wasn't at its best, instead of allowing the idea that other people in that room noticed my flaws to persist in my mind, I would change it to a different idea. I would say, "I am beautiful, people are staring at me because I look amazing today." Choosing to change my interpretation of others' glances changed my experience at the event, and as a result I enjoyed myself without allowing my mind to rob me of having a good time. We have no way of truly knowing what a person is thinking when they look our way, so why not choose to perceive the look as something coming from a positive place. Isn't that a more pleasant option.? Now, if I am concerned about an event I'm about to attend, I take a few minutes to meditate and visualize the exact way I want things to turn out. I create situations in my mind that make me feel loved. For example, I imagine everyone telling me how amazing I look and how gorgeous my dress is. In my mind, I create the entire day just as I desire it to be. If I want to be the center of attention, then I create that scenario in my mind. Taking the time to practice these imagination techniques makes it so much easier for me to enter the room. It's our world and we create our realities.

I remember being terribly nervous about giving a speech for my Eastern Star organization. Although I had been speaking professionally for a few years, this speech had me quite unsettled. I was the current Grand OES Queen for the year 2017 of the Golden State Grand Chapter, Order of the Eastern Star, Prince Hall Rite of Adoption for the state of California. This was my going-out queen speech. The crowning of the new queen would take place later that day. Because I had not felt completely embraced by some of the women in the organization, I was terribly afraid to deliver this speech. Most of the members had never heard me speak before, so I just didn't know what to expect. Being the determined person I am, I would not back out no matter how uneasy I felt. The day before my speech, I did nothing but visualize the outcome I desired. I closed my eyes and saw myself on stage in my beautiful white queen dress and sparkly queen's crown, delivering a magnificent, inspirational speech. I created the image of the audience in my mind. I visualized the event going exactly as I wanted it to. In my visual, the audience members were smiling and clapping, fully receiving the message I was delivering, even laughing at my jokes. Creating that visual helped me tremendously. If there were any non-supportive people in the audience, I didn't even notice them. I chose to design the room the way I wanted it to be and lived completely in my desired image of the moment and the moment became a reality. It all worked out perfectly! Creative visualization works! The ability to believe in things unseen is a tool God gave to us. The speech was a great success. I'd honestly had more fun that day as the outgoing queen than I did as the incoming queen.

It truly is all in the mind. Everything begins and ends there. Most of the situations we fear and torment ourselves with never actually happen anywhere but in our own minds. We have all been guilty of this, but it is time to fully understand the damage we do to our lives by allowing these negative thinking patterns to continue. Ask yourself why we tend to think about failure, death and tragedy far more often than they actually happen. We must learn to catch our mind when it is stuck focusing on imaginary situations that are not positive. Earl Nightingale said, *"Whatever we plant into our subconscious mind and nourish with repetition and emotion will become a reality".*

It may seem difficult at first to monitor every single thought, but it will eventually become second nature. Practicing it daily will make it easier and effortless eventually. I have been doing it for so long now my mind instantly begins reciting positive affirmations as soon as I wake up. Soon you will see your entire life change. The mind is amazing, and once you realize that the true key to happiness, success, great health, wealth, and all the love you desire all start with the mind, you will become dedicated to monitoring and manipulating your thoughts.

Practice it as you would anything in your life that you want to master. I create mental exercises regularly to help hone my creative visualization skills.

Start with simple ones. If you are dating someone who you sincerely want to marry. Create a visual of them standing at the altar waiting for you with a huge smile on their face. Imagine them walking toward you with a loving gaze, eager to become your life partner. Visualize your friends and family hugging you and your new spouse after the wedding during the reception. Imagine them all smiling and wishing the newly married couple well. Then imagine a happy marriage. Literally create mental images of the two of you celebrating your fifth,tenth and twenty-fifth anniversary. Design the entire relationship exactly the way you desire it to be. If you want your mate to give you lavish gifts several times a year, create that picture in your mind. Imagine a huge smile on your face as you graciously thank him/her for the gifts. Allow yourself to actually feel the feelings of gratitude while receiving them. These mental exercises work.

Commit to five minutes twice a day to intentionally creating positive images in your head. The image will become clearer and clearer each time. Once you have mastered the visual, add emotion to it. Emotion is the icing on the cake. Try to feel the way you would feel if this was actually happening. Combine the visual with the emotion and you have a perfect recipe for manifestation. Conscious, positive thought combined with feeling and emotion are the *real secret* to creating a great life.

@In59Seconds

Limitations are illusions. The only limits that truly exist are the ones you accept in your mind.
-SaBrina Fisher Reece

Three

Imagine It

One of the most precious gifts God gave us other than life is our ability to imagine. God gave us the ultimate control over the outcome of our lives through our imagination. I realize that initially it's a hard concept to grasp, but it's true. If we can imagine it, we can have it. It is through the use of these amazing imaginations of ours that we can live our best lives.

When you watch small children closely, you will see that they possess the untainted ability to imagine. They play for hours on end with people we can't see. They invent them in their minds, and if we truly watch them, it seems natural to them to create these playmates. I believe it is our natural ability to create, believe in, and interact with the unseen. As we age, we grow further and further away from our natural instincts. It seems to be the one missing piece from most lives. Like me, most people have no idea that their imagination has the power to create. I definitely did not know that when I was younger, nor did I have the slightest clue that I had any control over what I imagined. I now know that we can change and manipulate that visual. I still catch myself when my mind gets stuck on a visualization that isn't positive. Many times, I'll imagine one of my kids getting hurt, or I will create negative conversations with people in my mind. The difference between the old me and the new me is once I realize I am creating that negativity in my mind,

I immediately stop it. That's the first step. I'll sometimes physically shake my head to rid my mind of the negative movie playing inside, and instead of berating myself for allowing the negative thought to happen, I applaud myself for catching it and casting it out. When I speak to others motivationally, I teach a "Catch and Cast" technique. Catch the negative thoughts and cast them out.

The gift of imagination is powerful. In our mind we can literally design the exact picture of the life we desire to live. Whatever we allow our minds to focus on will eventually transform into matter and become tangible. Just try it! Take five minutes daily and focus on having a new car. In your mind's eye, design the vehicle to the very last detail. See the color, the make and model with every detail you want. Imagine everything from the steering wheel to the tires. Visualize the color of the seats and the carpet on the floor. Then imagine yourself sitting in it smiling, feeling so grateful for this new, beautiful car.

The magic of creation happens when we combine the image we have created with the emotion of receiving it. Neville Goddard said,

"Imagination is the very gateway of reality."

We must practice using our imagination in a positive way. Do this daily, even if it's for only a few minutes, and you will improve your life. The amount of time that it takes the things you desire to manifest is determined by how quickly you are able to completely remove doubt from the visuals you are creating. Doubt and fear counteract the manifestation. Pretend that you have it already. Believe that it exists in the present time and it will. I'm positive this is what the Bible was referring to in the scripture, *"Believe in things unseen as if they already are."*

Often, you will hear someone who has attained success in some area say, "I never imagined that this would happen to me." I'd like to challenge them by convincing them that it would not be happening had they not imagined it. At some point they must have held that thought in their mind for it to take root and grow into reality. The president of the United States would not have become president had he not mentally seen himself in that position. Singers would not be on stage singing had they not once visualized themselves there. The thoughts that we focus on are the ones that manifest into reality. It is important that we intentionally imagine the life we desire. Recognize the imagination for the gift of creation that it is.

Keep in mind, your imagination can bring your negative thoughts into reality as well. Try not to spend an extended amount of time imagining bad things. When you notice that you are daydreaming and it's not a good dream, stop it in its tracks and intentionally imagine something that makes you happy. We have so many unfounded subconscious fears that we don't realize how much we sit and think about things like death, car accidents, heartache, etc. Make sure your positive thoughts outweigh your negative. God gave us the power to bring things into existence. Make sure the things you bring into your life are good things.

Once you finally accept you do have this power, you will be more mindful of monitoring your thinking patterns. I can't say it's easy to continuously monitor your thoughts, but it will prove to be worth the effort and eventually it will become easier to do. Anything you do daily will become a habit. It should be everyone's goal to make positive thinking a habit.

Consider the quiet times you have to just sit and breathe and access your thoughts as a gift, because a gift is exactly what these moments are; a wonderful opportunity to take charge and be solely responsible for your happiness. We spend years blaming others for how our lives turn out, but rarely do we take responsibility for not making use of our divine God-given power to design a better life. Accepting this power does not negate the hurt that we have suffered at the hands of others. It doesn't erase injustices or minimize inequalities in the world. It simply frees us from the bondage of being a victim to the pain and trauma we have endured for the rest of our lives.

I don't believe in classifying people as good or bad because there is negative and positive in us all. However, this amazing power to create and manifest our desires is not only given to those the world perceives as good. Mind Magic is for everyone. We can choose to use it for good or evil. Keep in mind that humans are subject to certain immutable laws, so if you use your power to create chaos or evil, it will come back to you. Like attracting like is a universal law of karma that we seem to have no control over. It's simple, the energy you put out into the universe will return to you.

On my journey for truth I have studied many different interpretations of Universal Law. Some say there are seven or eight. Some say ten to fourteen with only a few of them being immutable. Immutable laws are the laws that we cannot change, such as gravity. Whether you are a good person or a bad person, if you decide to jump off of a building, due to the immutable law of gravity, you will go down and most likely not survive the fall. According to Newton, "What goes up, must come down." We don't know why this is, but as it stands it's a reality and a law we can't change.

Universal Laws are laws that were not made by man. They are laws that govern our universe:

15 Universal Laws

- The Law of Oneness
- The Law of Vibration
- The Law of Gravity
- The Law of Action (Action is energy in motion)
- The Law of Cause and Effect (Every action has a reaction or consequence)
- The Law of Correspondence (As above, so below; As within so without)
- The Law of Compensation
- The Law of Attraction (Like attracts like)
- The Law of Perpetual Transmutation of Energy (We have the power to change the energy in our lives)
- The Law of Gestation (Everything has its time to manifest)
- The Law of Relativity (Each person will receive challenges to strengthen them, it's all relative)
- The Law of Polarity (Everything has an opposite)
- The Law of Rhythm (Everything vibrates and moves)

- The Law of Belief (What you believe with thought & emotion will become reality)
- The Law of Gender (Yin & Yang; everything has masculine and feminine energy)

Some believe there are only seven universal laws. These are the seven deemed most important. These laws are also referred to as the "Seven Hermetic Laws" in the Kybalion.

7 Laws Universal Laws

1. The Law of Mentalism (Everything is mental. Everything originates from universal mind)
2. The Law of Correspondence (As above, so below; As within, so without. There is harmony and agreement between the spiritual and physical realms)
3. The Law of Attraction (We are magnets, and we attract everything that matches our intention and the energy we emit)
4. The Law of Polarity (Everything is dual. All truths are but half-truths, opposites are the same, but vary in degree,)
5. The Law of Rhythm (Everything flows, rises and falls)
6. The Law of Cause and Effect (Karma; For every action there is a consequence)
7. The Law of Gender (Gender manifests on all planes. Within every woman lies all the latent qualities of a man, and visa versa)

It took me years to fully understand these laws and even longer to decide that I believed in them, but they answer a lot of questions we have in life. Times when things just seem to happen no matter what we do. When we realize we are all subjected to these universal laws, things make a little more sense. I began to study the Law of Polarity, realizing that all opposites exist simultaneously. I made a point to be more intentional on which side of the pole I wanted to operate on. It also made me less judgmental in labeling others as either good or bad. I realized how close we all are to the opposite and how easily we can cross the center and move and operate on the other side of the pole. It all comes down to a choice. Good or bad, right or wrong, love or hate, we choose how we want to be.

We may try to be positive, but sometimes anger can cause us to swing to the opposite side and become negative. It's a choice to what degree and for how long we stay on the other side of the pole, but understanding polarity helps you see that we all start in the center. We choose to advance to one side or the other. And even when we swing to the less favorable side we can always come back.

It's also quite comforting once you fully understand the Law of Rhythm. You realize that when things seem low they will rise. There is a natural eb and flow. According to this law, all things rise and fall. This law is helpful when trying to understand the importance of balance. During times in your life when all seems to be going haywire, take comfort in knowing that according to the universal law of rhythm, things will get better. These Laws are things that may take what seems like a lifetime to comprehend, but I'm committed to doing so because all things mental, physical, and spiritual appear to be connected. And understanding that connection can lead to a more harmonious life.

When I was younger and knew nothing of vibration or frequency. I'm sure I was always vibrating low. I would get angry and sad a lot. I suffered from depression, and I had no idea I had any control over how I felt. Knowing the things I know now could have definitely minimized my suffering as a young adult. Now, I rarely find myself in those dark places. It's not that the feelings of sadness and despair don't show up periodically. I simply know exactly what to do to immediately get rid of them, or as I now refer to it, "raise my vibration." In January 2020, I appeared on a court television show. After it aired in March, I received a lot of ridicule and cruelty via social media.

I was devastated at the amount of hurtful messages I received, attacking everything from my personal appearance to my confident demeanor on the show. I could not believe the people went out of their way to contact me with the intent to be negative. The plaintiff and I both were given a fair shot at presenting our cases, and I won the case, fair and square. What was all the negative backlash about? Her dishonest testimony in court resulted in the judge not awarding her one cent. Her negative response later that day online sincerely caught me off guard. I was deeply hurt by the comments and for a minute I began to question my own beauty. My confidence was shaken. I remember walking to a mirror several times, internalizing all of their negative comments wishing I had not read them. I knew this was not positive, yet I had allowed it to get to me and it lowered my vibration. This situation gave me a lot of compassion for celebrities or people in the public eye. No one deserves public ridicule and it is very hurtful. As the world adapts quickly into a virtual society we must learn the art of encouraging ourselves daily so we don't not fall susceptible to online bullies.

I still cry when my feelings are hurt. I guess I just can't understand cruelty. This obvious sensitivity I have to it makes me stay mindful and make sure I do not treat anyone in a cruel way. I think every person should attempt to be kind to others. No one is perfect and we all have days where our spirits are low. However, please make it a point even during those times to be gentle and loving with yourself and others.

Now of course I know the damage of staying in that emotionally low place, so despite the fact that my feelings were deeply hurt and my self-esteem was greatly affected, I had to get up and do the work needed to bring myself back. I needed to speak positive affirmations to myself aloud and in a mirror. I had to encourage myself, as I teach my readers to do, and remind myself of my greatness. It would be great if we were all so evolved that we never allowed the opinions of others to affect us. It sounds good, but we still reside in a human body and can still be emotionally affected by others despite the abundance of mental and emotional work many of us have done. The great thing is, once we have armed ourselves with empowerment tools and the knowledge of how to use them we can always implement positive affirmations, meditation, effective prayer, and creative visualization to rebuild our confidence and return to love. And as hard as it may be, send positive energy and love to those that have harmed you because they are still part of the divine source. God loves them as much as he does you.

Clairaudience

In some way we are all connected spiritually. The idea of being connected to God, the Divine source of us all is quite comforting to me. I have come to believe we all have been given spiritual gifts from God. I can't say I fully understand their purpose, or how they enhance our lives, but I am now certain that I too have a gift. I am not positive, but I believe my spiritual gift is called clairaudience. I realize that some people may find this weird, but these things actually happen to me. On four separate occasions in my life, I have heard clearly and audibly recognizable voices that were not actually there.

1st time: I was twenty-one and my grandmother who raised me from three months to seventeen years old had been killed a few years prior. I was sleeping soundly when I heard her voice say, "Brina." I sat up in my bed peacefully and was so certain that it was her voice. There was no doubt who it was. I didn't for one second think it was anyone else. It was definitely the voice of my grandmother. Surprisingly I was not startled or afraid as many may have been from hearing the voice of a loved one who had passed on. I felt a sense of peace from the voice, and she was the only person in the world, even to this day that calls me Brina. I felt comforted so I lay back down and went back to sleep and never heard her voice again.

2nd time: I was forty-nine years old in 2019. I had been working really hard for the past three days and was sleeping unnaturally hard. I was in that stage of sleep where you're almost awake, but not quite. I clearly and very audibly heard my two youngest children in their room, adjacent to mine, trying to kill something that was on the wall. I don't know if it was a mosquito or what, but I heard them hitting the broom on the wall. I heard Journey, who was five years old at the time, scream to JJ, "Kill it! Did you get it?" I went back to sleep for a few more hours. When I woke up, I called JJ(Jayden) into my room. "What was it you were trying to kill ?" I asked her.

She said, "Huh?" I said, "I heard you and Journey in the room. You guys were making a lot of noise trying to kill something on the ceiling or wall. I heard the broom hitting the ceiling. Journey was screaming "Kill it."

She said, "Mom that was three days ago, and you weren't even home when it happened."

How was I able to tap into the audio of an incident that actually happened in my house three days prior, when I was not even there? How is that possible?

3rd Time: The day my oldest daughter Joi and her family moved to Arizona on Saturday, March 28th 2020. I was doing fine. I had months to accept the fact that she was moving, so I was not as emotionally upset as I expected myself to be, being that she was moving away with my infant first grandchild. We got them all packed and she and her husband and baby left to start their new lives. The evening came and I went to bed. When I woke up that morning, I clearly heard my grandson, Raiden crying as he normally does in the morning. I text Joi and said, "I just heard Raiden crying." She confirmed all the way from Arizona via text that he had just been crying before I texted her.

4th time: April 1, 2020. I was sleeping soundly, because I had been awake from midnight until 4:00 a.m. I woke up by what sounded like Joi walking into my room, saying, "Mom." She sounded sick, like she was coming to tell me she didn't feel good. I Instantly woke up! I texted my daughter in Arizona and asked if she was okay. She jokingly texted back; "Mom tell the ghost in the house to leave you alone."

After the fourth incident I began to study even more spiritual books and videos. I learned that most people have spiritual gifts, but it is our choice whether to ignore these gifts or embrace and develop them. I am still unsure what purpose these gifts have for showing up in our lives but I'm curious to find out. I only want to develop my spiritual gift of clairaudience if it will help me and those close to me advance in some positive way. I have no desire to hear voices for no reason. if it can serve some positive purpose in my life then I'm all for it.

There is one irrefutable certainty in this life. We will all die. Each and every one of us, no matter what great physical condition we are in, or how much energy we have put into gaining wealth and success. We will all leave this life experience at some point. Accepting this makes it easier for me to concern myself less with *how, when, and why.* Instead, I choose to focus on making sure I leave a significant legacy. I want my children to be able to pick up one of my books and share the beliefs and concepts that were important to me with others. I want them to remember that I taught them that they are creators, and that they are responsible for their own lives. I want them to know the importance of loving themselves first. I want them to create opportunities for themselves and to not accept any limitations. Before I leave this Earth, it is my duty as a parent to make sure they understand that people are not as limited as they sometimes believe they are. They can have whatever life they desire, and I would like to ensure they possess the tools needed to acquire it.

Yes, there are many things we all can do to extend our life experience, but knowing that no matter what, it will end one day should make us all want to commit to making sure we figure out what our true purpose here is, and direct all of our energy toward pursuing it. While pursuing your purpose, make happiness your mission. Enjoy every moment of this beautiful life experience.

Four

Monitor Your Mindset

For us to become aware of our thoughts we first need to slow our lives down a bit. We must take advantage of quiet moments and be still long enough to monitor our thoughts. When you are sitting in traffic, turn the radio off, take a few deep breaths, and begin to notice and acknowledge every thought that comes into your mind. Learning to do this changed my life tremendously. Both good and bad thoughts need recognition. You cannot reverse negative thoughts if you have not taken the time to recognize and acknowledge they exist. Begin by keeping it as simple as taking a mental note of what you are thinking. Start by observing exactly what you are thinking right now. Take ten minutes and detach from everything in the world except your thoughts.

Make a conscious decision to do this every day and, eventually you will see the clear distinction between intentional thoughts versus when our mind runs rampant on its own without any guidance from us. Only then will you notice how many thoughts of fear and impending tragedy run through our minds. These are specifically the thoughts we must learn to dismiss. These are the thoughts that will ultimately cause us harm. It's not horrible to admit you have negative thoughts, on the contrary, it's the first step to a better life. Many will spend years in complete denial. Denying they are even capable of thinking negatively. Negative thoughts exist, just like crime, and while we may not be able to control the crime in the world, we have the power to monitor our thoughts. Stop judging your thoughts as good or bad and re-label them as "thoughts that make you feel good" or "thoughts that make you feel bad." Choosing to label them as good or bad will make you less likely to acknowledge the ones that are not in line with what you desire for your life. Denial and embarrassment will slow down the process. We all think negatively at times. No need to guilt yourself for being a bad thinker. We all have thoughts of fear, failure, anger, sickness, and sadness. You are not alone. You are not a bad person for thinking that way. However, now that you are aware of the damage sustaining a negative thinking pattern can do to your life, it's time to change it. Feel good about being at a place in your life where you are willing to make positive changes towards the betterment of your future. This is the best gift you can give to yourself and others. Learning how to control and change your thoughts will change your life. As human beings we can get so distracted by the ins and outs of our daily routines that most of us rarely even realize that we are thinking all day. Scientists say we have twelve to sixty thousand thoughts per day.

Thoughts come continuously, whether or not we choose to guide them. These thoughts are shaping our daily lives so we must learn to take charge of them. You are what you think all day long. There is no way around it. Our realities are shaped solely by our thoughts. If it's present in our lives, even if we don't remember those specific thoughts, we did indeed think them. We have to learn to create barriers to keep the negative thoughts from penetrating our subconscious mind. We can't avoid thinking, so it's best we take control over this imminent process and manipulate it in our favor. All thoughts travel on energetic frequencies. We are energy as well. Everything in this world is energy, and we have the power to control the energy we put out. Energy exists, no matter what, but we can determine if the energy we emit is positive or negative. If we are entertaining thoughts of disease because someone we know was just diagnosed with an illness and we are now in fear of getting it, then rest assured that our energetic vibration is low at that time.

The good thing is we are in control of the level of energy we put out. We can raise our own energetic vibration at any time. A friend of mine taught me about saging a few years ago. At that point in my life, I was open to new ideas and concepts regarding religion and spirituality. She brought a small piece of sage to my salon and showed me how to use it. I am a person that knows the importance of "belief" in something, so as she was showing me how to rid my body and private spaces of negative energy that can lurk in corners and dark spaces, I set a conscious intention to not reject what she was saying simply because it was foreign to me. Even though it was different and conflicted with my childhood Christian beliefs, I tried to listen and learn with an open mind. I decided that day that the practice of saging was no different than the Christian ritual of taking communion. The drinking of the grape juice and eating of the cracker is also a ritual in remembrance of Jesus Christ and his bodily sacrifice. Communion is a ritual that Christians chose to assign symbolism to. Unfortunately, it was my experience growing up in COGIC (Church Of God in Christ) that only our rituals were accepted, and everything else was considered voodoo or witchcraft. I no longer believe that. I can't say I ever personally bought into the voodoo concept; it was simply the belief of many of the elders that came before me. Most were devout Christians and would have never accepted the belief in healing crystals, burning sage and meditation to open our chakras. Chakras are the centers of spiritual power in the human body. After my friend was gone I decided to practice what she taught me about saging. I also chose to envision the dark energy leaving through a window and the positive energy coming in. I would say "Negative energy out, positive energy in." As I walk around my salon burning the sage and setting my intentions for positivity and prosperity, I would close my eyes and believe it all as fact. What you believe is what truly matters. You can practice certain rituals but inside you have no faith in them, so they won't work. Many people believe the art of rituals and spiritual ceremonies are evil and demonic. My response to people who say that to me is "That's not what it means to me". Do not allow other people to assign an intention to something you choose to do. For example I am a mother of four and I would allow my children to dress up in customs for Halloween and take part in the parade at school. We would even go from house to house trick- or treating in the evening.

Frequently people have reminded me of some ancient original demonic meaning the Halloween holiday. It never bothered me one bit because that is not what me and my children celebrate it for. We have no evil intent behind our choice to celebrate the holiday nor are we bound by anyone else's. There is always someone who chooses to corrupt something. I choose to see the positive in all things. And any holiday that promotes love and brings people and families closer is OK with me. The choice to participate in something evil is just that, a choice. I'm not interested, and it has nothing to do with me. The practice of saging became a regular practice in my salon, Braids By SaBrina, which has been my sole source of income for twenty-five years. In September 2019, I changed the name of my salon to "A New Vision Dreadlock Studio." One would think changing the name of a popular business that had serviced the Los Angeles community for so long would not be a great idea, but I sat in stillness for a while and the new name suddenly came to me in less than fifteen minutes. I was fifty years old.

I had recently dealt with some unexpected medical issues that caused me to rethink allowing any form of stress in my life. My staff at my salon were a key source of stress, and at this point there wasn't much of a financial benefit to keeping them around. I felt I had given all that I could to them over the years and now I had to make myself and my health a priority. I made an instant decision to terminate them and change the name of the salon to "A New Vision Dreadlock Studio." It was a new day and time for A New Vision as I embarked upon the second half of my life.

To this day, I have never regretted my decision. The new salon name came to me so peacefully that I knew it was God telling me to move forward. When we spend time with our mind we will discover answers to questions, solutions to problems will be revealed to us. I started sitting quietly in the empty salon; something I was never able to do when I had employees. I would visualize abundant wealth, and thank God for continued success. I spoke aloud words of gratitude for my business and how consistent it had been. Then I would walk from room to room, saging my beautiful purple salon and speaking my affirmations for both my business and myself aloud. I raised my personal prices considerably and within thirty days of re-branding my salon, I was making double what I made before, even without having a staff. It turned out to be one of the best decisions I have ever made.

Wealth and success can become a reality for anyone who sincerely believes it is possible. I believe that is why I have never experienced poverty. I expect wealth, and yes, I advertise and do all the footwork needed to sustain a small business, but that to me is secondary. My belief that the business could not fail was the primary cause of its continued success. Advertising and promoting a business won't work if subconsciously you believe it will fail. We must see the success in our mind first. God gave us this power as a gift to mankind, but most do not use it. You can experience success in all areas of your life if you first believe it to be possible. All things are possible!. This new practice of saging was just another tool I used to set intentions for peace and prosperity in my life.

There is not one specific tool. Any practice you put complete unwavering belief in will be successful. I'm pleased that I opened my mind and allowed myself to at least listen to other concepts and beliefs and make my own choices. Having that open mind allowed me to be more receptive when I traveled to Bali, Indonesia, Cusco, Peru, Cairo, Egypt, Istanbul, Turkey, and Athens, Greece. In these countries, I visited many monasteries and spiritual temples, which helped to strengthen my belief in one Divine Source.

Different people may package God differently. They may refer to God with a different name, but to me, it's all the same. I respect the amount of reverence that other countries give to honor the creator. I have partaken in many rituals and ceremonies that greatly differ from my Christian church practices. What I've learned is to allow others to worship God the way they choose. It's not my business. If there was a particular practice that resonated with me, I adopted it as my own and moved forward. I feel we get so distracted in pointing out the different way in which we all choose to acknowledge God.

Our ego wants us to be correct. It convinces us that our way is the only way. It's a distraction and a judgment that I don't believe in. To each his own. Who are we to say how another person should acknowledge God? The ultimate universal goal is to live a great life. Learning, growing and evolving in all areas and allowing others to do the same. I do, however, believe that once we fully evolve we don't necessarily need to practice daily rituals to remind us to be positive and speak positivity over our lives. By then, the positive thought process will have become second nature. However, until then, the daily practices that help us keep a positive mental attitude are crucial to having a productive life. They help us form positive daily habits. I was proud that I was able to open my mind and embrace practices that were a definite step out of the C.O.G.I.C. box I was raised in. I have gotten to a point where I enjoy them. I believe strongly in them. I believe they are necessary, and I look forward to doing them daily. I still believe very much in Jesus Christ. I believe he was here to teach us of our Amazing internal power.

I believe that power is what he was referring to as "The Kingdom of Heaven" with-in us all. I will always be eternally grateful for my Christian upbringing. Unlike most I see correlations between Christianity and spirituality. I combine what practices and beliefs work best for my life and move forward. I have convinced myself that taking that small time out of my day to speak positivity over my body, my family, my business, and my life in general is truly the reason I no longer suffer from many of the things a lot of people in this world currently suffer with. I want to teach others how I rid my life of sadness, pain, hopelessness and depression. I get so excited about teaching these practices to others because it is my desire for everyone to learn that their happiness is a choice, and choosing to spend just a little time with your mind can ensure you live a better life.

As far as we know, we only get one mind. Spend as much time with it as possible. View your mind as the cockpit of an airplane. With all the controls clearly accessible and you are the pilot

@In59Seconds

Forgiveness frees the heart and mind, and prepares you for greatness.

Five

Energy

I realize your definition of "energy" may be related to how hyper or mobile you think you are, or how fast you can pop up, get ready for work, or rush to that morning workout class. But this book will teach you about different kinds of energy. The invisible yet powerful frequency that shapes everything in our lives. This book will show you that everything is Energy and Energy is Everything.

When I say "Everything," I mean everything. The chair you sit in. The desk at work. Your coffee cup. Your computer, the rock outside. The trees in the park. The tomatoes in your garden. Even your thoughts. Yep, your unseen thoughts are energy. It's all made up of vibrating particles, constantly moving, even when they appear still.

Once I learned this concept, I began to pay attention to what we often consider inanimate objects, especially the beautiful flowers and trees. I took comfort in realizing they have their own form of intelligence and vibration.

31

Each petal, each leaf, each branch dances in its own energetic rhythm. Now I am constantly pointing out beautiful trees to my kids as we are driving. Having lived in the same community for 30 years, I'm positive I have driven past these trees many times and never noticed their beauty. I just took a trip to New Mexico, and I was in awe of how mesmerizing the fall trees were.

Now, I must admit, it's a little harder to accept that a chair, table, ink pen, or comb is also energy, but it is. Everything is made of the same divine substance: light vibrating at different speeds, and that includes money. Everything has the beautiful spirit of God in it, not just human beings.

Now let's get technical for a min:

Webster's dictionary defines energy as a qualitative attribute describing a system's capacity to perform work, with definitions ranging from inherent power and vigor to the quantifiable ability to do work in physics.

Google describes energy as a fundamental concept in physics that exists in various forms, such as kinetic (motion), potential (stored), thermal (heat), and chemical energy. For example, when you lift a book, you give it potential energy, and as it falls, that energy converts to kinetic energy, demonstrating its capacity to cause change.

I am aware that those definitions seem quite complicated. I agree. I choose initially to keep it simple. Energy is the unseen force in everything. When we wake up in the morning and we feel literal excitement about the day, that feeling is energy. When someone upsets us and we verbally scream, that action is energy. When we hand the cashier a dollar bill, we are transferring energy.

Spiritual Energy: Spiritual energy is described by Google as the unseen life force connecting everything, felt as internal sensations, emotions, or a universal current representing our vitality, purpose, and connections to God.

Whether we understand and agree with those definitions or not, we cannot deny that we have all felt some form of energy throughout our lives. After reading this book, you will start to recognize the different types of energy in your lives.

Energy is the invisible thread that weaves together the fabric of existence. It flows through galaxies and blades of grass, through storms, laughter, sunlight, and thought. Everything that exists, seen or unseen, is made of energy. Modern science calls it matter in motion. Spirituality calls it life force, but it's definitely undeniable.

Though they speak in different languages, both science and spirit agree: energy never dies. It merely transforms. Bare with me through the technical terms, please..

Thermal Energy - The Fire of Life

The warmth you feel from the sun, the heat that keeps your body alive, that's thermal energy. It's the motion of particles, vibrating faster as temperature rises. In thermodynamics, energy can neither be created nor destroyed, it can only change form. Spiritually, this mirrors our own eternal essence. The energy that animates your body is not lost when you die; it simply transitions, just as ice becomes water, and water becomes vapor.

Kinetic Energy - The Energy of Motion

Every heartbeat, every dance, every ocean wave carries kinetic energy, movement. It's the science of motion, but it's also a metaphor for spiritual flow. When we resist life, we stagnate. When we move with grace, faith, and trust, energy flows freely through us, propelling us toward growth.

Potential Energy - The Power Within

Potential energy is sacred energy in waiting, the quiet pulse of possibility held within us all. Like a coiled spring before release or an arrow drawn back, it symbolizes the divine potential resting inside every soul. Spiritually, it mirrors the Creator's power within us, the dormant vibration of faith, love, creativity, and healing that awakens when belief and intention align.

In my spare time, I paint (#SpiritualArtFromMyHeart). My friends often call me creative, but I always smile and tell them, we all are. Creativity is not reserved for a chosen few; it is the divine current that flows through all of us. Some have simply not tapped into it yet and discovered how to let it flow.

Electromagnetic Energy - The Language of the Universe

Light, sound, radio waves, Wi-Fi, all of them are electromagnetic energy. You can't see it, yet you use it every day. Spiritually, this mirrors the unseen ways in which we communicate energy, thoughts, emotions, and prayers. When you think lovingly of someone, that thought travels like a wave, touching their field. Science calls it resonance; spirit calls it connection.

Chemical Energy - The Spark of Creation

Inside every cell, chemical reactions transform food into life force. It's the alchemy of biology, divine chemistry at work. When you eat, breathe, and love, energy is exchanged. Scientists say the molecules of your body come from stars that exploded billions of years ago. You are, quite literally, stardust reorganized by divine intelligence.

Gravitational Energy - The Force of Connection

Gravity keeps the planets in orbit and our feet on the ground. But beyond physics, it carries a deeper message, it represents spiritual grounding, the sacred pull that keeps us connected to the Earth, to one another, and to God.

As my spiritual journey deepened, I began to truly understand the importance of grounding, or earthing, as some call it. Whenever I can, I step into my backyard, slip off my shoes, and press my bare feet into the grass. I can literally feel the energy of the Earth rise to meet me. The ground hums beneath me, steady and alive, reminding me that healing and balance are never far, they are right beneath our feet.

Gravity, in both the physical and spiritual sense, reminds us that everything is held in divine balance. Nothing drifts away from its purpose. Even when we feel untethered, the unseen hand of creation keeps us anchored to what matters most, love, truth, and the present moment.

When we ground ourselves, we reconnect with God's rhythm moving through the Earth. The same divine energy that holds the planets in orbit also flows through the soil beneath our feet. Each time we touch the Earth with intention, we realign our frequency with nature.

Grounding is more than standing barefoot in the grass; it's remembering where we come from. It's a spiritual recalibration that reminds us that no matter how high we rise, we are still of the Earth, divinely supported and sustained by it. When life feels chaotic or uncertain, grounding draws us back into balance, mind, body, and spirit.

The Earth is a living teacher. Its pulse beats in harmony with our own, and when we take a moment to listen, we hear the whisper of God in the wind, the rhythm of creation in the soil, and the peace that comes from simply being still.

Spiritual Energy - The Breath of God

Every tradition has a name for it: Chi, Prana, Holy Spirit, Life Force. It's the subtle energy that sustains all life, unseen but deeply felt.

Prayer warriors call upon this spiritual energy. Reiki healers channel it. Meditators feel it as tingling warmth. It's the divine frequency that moves through everything alive. When you pray or meditate, you align your field with this sacred current, allowing healing and inspiration to flow through you.

Air - The Invisible Force of Presence

Air is the most immediate form of energy we experience yet often overlook. Breath is sacred. Each inhale carries oxygen that ignites the fire of life within you. Each exhale releases what no longer serves. Spiritually, breathing is a daily reminder that energy is always flowing, giving and receiving, expanding and contracting.

Emotional Energy — The Frequency of Feeling

Emotions are energetic signals, vibrations that communicate with the body and the universe. Love vibrates high, radiating expansion and attraction. Fear vibrates low, creating contraction and limitation. When we manage our emotions, we manage our frequency. When we practice gratitude, forgiveness, and compassion, we lift our energetic signature to match divine flow.

Conscious Energy, The Creator Within

Human consciousness is the most powerful energy of all. Thoughts are frequencies that organize matter. Every belief you hold sends a signal to the universe. As Jesus said, "It is done unto you as you believe." When we consciously direct thought with love, gratitude, and faith, we co-create reality. When we dwell in fear or doubt, we lower our vibration and block divine flow.

"Everything is energy and that's all there is to it. Match the frequency of the reality you want and you cannot help but get that reality."
-Albert Einstein

The concept of energy may seem mystical, but it's measurable, felt, and undeniably real, yet its source is profoundly sacred. God, or the Universal Source, is the eternal field from which all energy flows. Every sunrise, every heartbeat, every thought is a ripple in that divine ocean. And every day, you wake with the opportunity to tune your frequency. Will you radiate peace or anger? Love or fear? Gratitude or worry?

God has already given us the tools, prayer, meditation, sunlight, laughter, music, touch, stillness, to raise our individual vibration and return to our natural state of harmony. We are not powerless spectators in our emotional lives. We have been given the ability to choose, moment by moment, what type of energy we want to emit into the world.

Many people believe they have no control over how they feel, but that belief is simply untrue. Even when a situation justifiably makes you angry, you still get to decide how long you remain in the energy of anger. You may not control the trigger, but you absolutely control the duration. Don't stay there long, because like attracts like. The energy you release is the energy that returns to you, magnified, multiplied, and mirrored back through people, situations, and circumstances.

When you understand this, you stop letting emotions possess you and start directing them. You stop surrendering your power to the moment and start exercising the authority God placed within you. Make no mistake, this is not an easy feat to attempt. I am speaking from experience.

I had been through so much in my early years that by age twenty-six, I had a bad temper. My temper was rooted in anger with God and fear of allowing anyone to get close enough to hurt me again. I was proud of my temper then. I was young and misinformed. I was impulsive, and my emotions ruled my life. Thank goodness I never got into any real trouble.

Eventually, I sought out help. I found a local anger management class and enrolled myself in it. That was the beginning of taking control over my life and learning how not to be so reactive. It was a start, just the first step, but it would be years before I truly figured it out.

Rage, anger, and explosive behavior may have a root cause, hurt, abandonment, childhood trauma could have been the catalyst, but we are still responsible for how we show up in the world. The things we have been through in the past should not be allowed to dictate our future. Healing does not erase the story, but it rewrites how the story shapes your life. Learning to guide your emotions, instead of letting them guide you, is one of the greatest forms of spiritual maturity.

Managing your energy isn't just emotional intelligence; it's **spiritual alignment**. Alignment, which many people assume is a New Age spiritual term, is actually a universal truth. Alignment means: your inner world, your beliefs, values, emotions, and intentions, matches your outer world, your actions, choices, words, and behavior. It is the state of being where what you *think*, what you *feel*, and what you *do* are moving in the same direction.

When you are aligned, you stop living in internal conflict. Your energy becomes clear and your prayers gain power. Your decisions become sharper, and the sooner you shift your frequency into alignment, the sooner your life begins to shift with it.

When we remember that we are energy, infinite, divine, and creative, we stop chasing power and start embodying it. We realize heaven isn't a place we go to; it's a frequency we rise to. It's the choice we make daily to show love and kindness and allow ourselves to feel it as well. We have the ability to create heaven right here on earth for ourselves.

At the core of everything, beneath flesh, thought, and matter, we are light, spiritual electricity animated by divine intelligence. That same spark that ignited the stars lives within each one of us. When we align with it, we become conscious co-creators of our reality. The more we honor that sacred energy through love, faith, and gratitude, the more we reflect the image of the God who created us all. Not metaphorically, but literally. Every cell in your body, every breath you take, every emotion you feel is made of vibrating particles moving so quickly that they appear solid to the naked eye. But if we could see the truth of what we are, we would witness light in motion, an astonishing, radiant frequency of consciousness expressing itself through form.

The human body is a beautiful vessel that God allows our spirit to hang out in, but we are **spiritual energy first**. That is the energy that continues when we die. The body returns to the earth, but the spirit returns to Source. Knowing this shifts everything. It reminds us that we are not confined by physical limits, emotional wounds, or the stories people told us about ourselves.

While we are here, we must realize that we have the ability to influence the type of life experience we have. We can choose how we show up in the world. We can choose what we focus on. We can choose the frequency we operate at, and if we are clearly operating at a low vibration, we can elevate it. We do not have to stay mad, sad or frustrated. Happiness is not left up to fate, it is a conscious daily decision, a vibrational stance, a spiritual choice to align with what is good, uplifting, and true.

Life does not just happen to you; you participate in its creation. The moment you recognize yourself as spiritual energy first, you stop waiting for circumstances to shift your mood and start shifting your energy to reshape your circumstances. The power lies with-in you.

Modern science confirms what ancient wisdom has always known: everything in existence vibrates. From the stars to the soil beneath our feet, to

38

the pulse inside your chest, life itself is a symphony of frequencies. Within this cosmic orchestra, *you* are both an instrument and a composer. We are energetic beings with the divine power to tune our vibration, to choose the frequency at which we live, love, and create.

When we "vibrate high," we align with the states of love, peace, happiness, and gratitude. Our energy feels light, magnetic, alive. When we "vibrate low," we resonate with fear, anger, jealousy, and scarcity. The air around us feels heavy; we attract more struggle and limitation because our internal frequency matches that field.

The spiritual and **metaphysical** truth is this: your energy determines your experience. The outer world mirrors the inner vibration. This is why two people can face the same challenge, yet one sees opportunity while the other sees defeat. Their energetic frequency shapes their perception, their reactions, and ultimately, their reality. From a **spiritual** standpoint, this is what the Bible means when it says, *"As a man thinketh in his heart, so is he."* It's not only about thought, it's about vibration. Your thoughts, emotions, and beliefs send out energetic signals, and the Universe, or what many call God, responds in perfect harmony.

God the amazing unseen force that created us all, has gifted us the divine ability to elevate our vibration. We are not prisoners of our moods or victims of our circumstances. Every single day, we are handed sacred tools to lift our frequency and reconnect with the flow of the Divine.

We do not have to remain in misery or sink into despair. The moment we choose to rise, the energy within us begins to shift. Healing starts with a decision, the decision to feel better, to reach higher, to tune back into love, to intentionally change our mood. Making these decisions changed the entire course of my life, and it will do the same for yours.

There isn't only one path to raise your vibration. Each soul finds its own rhythm. For me, it's gospel music or the soothing resonance of my crystal sound bowls. For someone else, it might be running, working out, going to church, reading scripture, or simply breathing in silence. What matters is the intention, the willingness to realign with peace. You choose which tools bring you joy and peace and make them daily rituals.

Don't get caught up in someone else's path; find your own. Don't allow other to tell you that your path is wrong. If it feels good and makes you happy, grounded, and content, you may be heading in the right direction. If it invokes kindness and love for yourself and others, then you are on the right path. But if the path you've chosen has you stressed, unhappy, tense, and irritated all the time, you may want to take a step back and rethink it. Your spirit will always reveal when something is not aligned.

Every sincere effort to uplift yourself, in whatever form it takes, is sacred. Do get caught up is the judgments of society. We should honor and respect all paths that lead toward light, for each one is another expression of God's love moving through us.

Sound is one of the oldest tools. Sound healing, chanting, or simply listening to music that stirs your soul, they all shift the energy field around and within you. Sound is vibration, and vibration is life. The right frequency can soothe the mind, heal the body, and open the heart. I love the concept of sound healing so much that I created a small sound meditation area in my salon. I offer individual Sound Meditation Session to some of my clients. #SoundWithSaBrina

The sun is another sacred source of energy. Its warmth and light nourish not only the earth but our spirit. Spending time in sunlight literally recharges your cells, elevates your mood, and reminds you that light is your natural state. Many times I'm looking for my daughter Jayden and can't find her. I then remember how much she loves to sit in the backyard in the sun. I always find her there.

Laughter is the highest vibration of joy. It breaks stagnant energy, restores balance, and invites divine flow. It's no coincidence that when we laugh, our entire body releases tension, our vibration instantly rises.

Meditation and **prayer** are gateways to energetic alignment. Meditation quiets the noise and brings your awareness back to the now, where God's energy is fully present. Prayer opens the heart, inviting guidance, gratitude, and connection with something greater than yourself.

These are not rituals of escape; they are acts of attunement. They are simply daily positive practices that make you feel better. They help you return to your natural state of love, which is one of the highest frequencies in the universe.

Although we appear to be solid matter, in truth, we are more space than substance. Beneath the atoms that make up our skin and bones lies pure potential, energy vibrating at different frequencies. The slower the vibration, the denser and heavier the form appears. The faster the vibration, the lighter, more ethereal, and radiant it becomes.

This is why we can feel energy long before words are spoken. Vibration transcends language, it communicates directly from soul to soul.

When my kids were teenagers, I could always sense when they had an attitude, even when they insisted, "Nothing's wrong." I could feel it, the tension in the air, the subtle shift in vibration. That invisible energy always spoke louder than their words. Plus a mother always knows lol.

You've likely felt it too, that unmistakable awareness when you walk into a room and instantly know whether there's love, peace, or anger lingering in the space. I haven't always been mature enough to ignore those obvious negative energies in certain rooms. There were times, especially early in my speaking career, when I could feel the energy shift the moment I was introduced. Not everyone was welcoming. Some faces silently asked, *"Who is she? Can she even speak?"*

I'm far more confident as a speaker now, but I've learned an important truth: you're not imagining what you feel. That energy is real. However, mastering vibration means learning not to let that energy control you. My job as a speaker was to motivate and uplift entire rooms, sometimes filled with over six hundred people. Even when I sensed doubt or judgment, I had to rise above it, channeling that energy into purpose. And every time I did, something beautiful happened, the same people who once questioned me would line up afterward to shake my hand, share their stories, and buy my books.

Make no mistake, frequency is real. Energy never lies; it introduces itself before a single word is said. When we become more aware of vibration, we begin to listen not just with our ears, but with our spirit. We learn to feel beneath the surface, to hear the silent language of energy that connects us all. Awareness of vibration is awareness of life itself, for energy is the first voice of creation.

God designed us as vibrational beings because creation itself is vibrational. The same divine frequency that birthed galaxies beats within your chest. And every morning, you have the sacred choice: to tune in to love or to fear, to radiate peace or carry chaos.

Raising your vibration isn't about pretending life is perfect, it's about remembering that *you are powerful energy in motion.* You are a child of the Divine Source, who I choose to call God, capable of creating harmony wherever you go. When you make the conscious choice to *Raise Your Personal Vibration* you then have the power to elevate the entire room.

So before you step into the world, take a moment to align your energy. Pray. Breathe. Smile. Step into sunlight. Let gratitude move through you like music. Because when you raise your frequency, you don't just change your day, you change the world around you.

Changing our Relationship with Money

Now lets talk about money, money is one of the most misunderstood forms of energy on the planet. We often attach so much fear, shame, or obsession to it that we distort its natural flow.

The very word currency comes from current, a flowing movement of energy. That alone tells us what money truly is: a circulating force meant to move, not to stagnate. Every time money passes from one hand to another, an **energetic exchange** occurs. Think about it, when you pay someone for their service, you're not just handing over paper. You're transferring gratitude, respect, and acknowledgment of value. When you receive money, you're also receiving energy, the vibration of appreciation, effort, and sometimes even the emotional frequency of the person it came from. That's why it's so important to cleanse your beliefs about money.

Your thoughts about it carry their own vibration. If you grew up hearing "money is the root of all evil" or "it's hard to come by," then that becomes the frequency you emit, and because the Universe always mirrors our energy, it reflects back exactly what we believe, be it scarcity or abundance. Money doesn't have feelings, but it responds to yours. If you constantly feel stressed or unworthy of financial comfort, money senses that vibration and stays away. But when you bless it, respect it, and view it as a divine tool to do good, it begins to flow more easily. When I receive money, even something as small as a few dollars, I take a moment to bless it. I say, "Thank you, God, for this energy of provision. I thank you in advance for it multiplying and returning to me and others tenfold." That small act of gratitude keeps my vibration open to abundance.

The key to financial peace isn't chasing money, it's raising your energy to match the frequency of abundance. Abundance is indeed real. There is truly more than enough money for us all. We simply must ensure that your relationship with money is positive. We must show gratitude for what we have been blessed with thus far. When you embody gratitude, generosity, and trust, you naturally become magnetic to prosperity. You no longer operate in desperation or limitation. You operate in faith and flow. Money will begin to flow to you easily and frequently. That is one of my personal affirmations I say daily. *"Money flows , easily and frequently into my life".*

We must also understand that the way we spend money carries energy too. If we spend from guilt, we vibrate low. But if we spend with joy, supporting businesses, artists, causes we believe in or hobbies we love, the energy of that exchange returns to us multiplied. Money is like love it grows where it is appreciated.

So, the next time you pay a bill, shift your energy from frustration to gratitude. Instead of complaining, whisper a quiet thank you: *"Thank you, God, that I have the resources to pay this."* You'll feel the difference instantly, because gratitude carries a vibration that attracts more to be grateful for.

I always remind my children, "Make sure to thank God for the pennies, nickels, and dimes just as much as the larger bills." It all matters. When you show appreciation for what seems small, you signal to the universe that you're ready for more. Gratitude multiplies everything it touches, it turns ordinary moments into blessings and lack into flow. Every act of gratitude opens new channels of abundance in my life. I am thankful for all that I have, and even more grateful for all that's on its way.

Remember, money mirrors your beliefs. Stop saying, "I can't afford that," or "I'm broke." Even on days when your bank account doesn't reflect abundance, remind yourself that this is only temporary. Speak words of increase, not lack. The moment you change the language you use around money, you begin to shift your energy toward it, and that shift opens new channels for it to flow into your life.

True abundance isn't just about money. In reality, money is only one small expression of a much greater vibration, the frequency of *more than enough*. When your thoughts, words, and emotions align with that truth, you begin to attract opportunities, peace, and prosperity in every form.

Real abundance is peace of mind. It's great health in your body. It's laughter with people you love. It's being so aligned with God's rhythm that your spirit feels full even when your bank account doesn't. So many people chase financial gain thinking it will fill the emptiness within them, but abundance isn't something you chase; it's something you *tune into*. It's a frequency that already exists inside you. When you vibrate at peace, gratitude, and trust, that energy radiates outward and draws everything you need toward you, relationships, opportunities, healing, and yes, financial blessings too. When you vibrate high, you stop operating from lack and limitation. You stop saying, "I don't have enough," and begin declaring, "I already am enough." Abundance in all areas of your life is definitely a possibility. It already exists in your life, you simply have to learn to vibrate on the same frequency that it does.

That one energetic shift changes everything. God never intended for us to live in a constant state of worry. The same divine source that designed oceans and galaxies designed *you,* with infinite potential and access to spiritual wealth. You can be rich in all areas of your life, if you believe you can. Scripture says, *"As a man thinketh in his heart, so is he."* That is not just scripture or poetic language; it's a metaphysical truth. Your internal vibration becomes your external experience.

When I began to see life this way, I realized that abundance flows in through every channel, not just in payments from my salon but in love and happiness all around. It can come through unexpected favor, new ideas, divine connections, or simply through an inner sense of joy that no one can take away.

Abundance is a mindset and **Mind is all**. It's the decision to see beauty where others see nothing. It's waking up grateful before anything even happens that day. When you live in that energy, you start to notice miracles in the smallest details, a smile from a stranger, a parking spot right in front, a friend calling at the perfect time. These are all reminders that the Universe is alive and responsive, and God is always on your side. True abundance is the realization that **you are already connected to everything you desire.**

You don't have to chase abundance, it's already yours. The goal isn't to fight for prosperity, but to *align* with it. Abundance responds to belief, not struggle. It's time to rewrite how we speak about prosperity and train our energy to match it. Try shifting your language like this:

✦ Instead of saying, **"I'm broke,"** affirm, **"I'm in transition."**

✦ Instead of saying, **"I can't afford it,"** declare, **"I'm creating the resources."**

✦ Instead of saying, **"I don't have enough,"** remind yourself, **"Everything I need is already here."**

As I always tell my friends Letty from Miami and Sapphire Moonbeam from Kansas City,

"It's already done." Remember the powerful truth: **Believe in things unseen as if they already are.**

✦ *Here are a few Money Affirmations:*

I am a divine magnet for abundance.
I move through life with gratitude, peace, and purpose.
Money flows to me easily and frequently into my life
I release fear, I trust in God, and I live in overflow.
I am Rich in all area of my life.
I live and vibrate on the same frequency of abundance.
I am connected to the endless flow of divine prosperity.
My wealth is not just in money, it's in peace, love, health, and happiness.
Everything I need is already within me.

Words are also energy, and every declaration either raises or lowers your vibration. So speak life over your finances, your dreams, and your relationships. Speak abundance. Speak peace. Speak joy. Speak God's light into everything you do. When you vibrate in gratitude, you stop chasing and start attracting. You stop begging and start believing it's already done. And that's when the miracles start to unfold.

When I look back over my life, I can see how my relationship with money and abundance has evolved right alongside my spiritual growth. In my younger years, I was always in survival mode, working hard, hustling seven days a week. When I opened my salon, *Braids by SaBrina*, I poured my entire heart and soul into it. I worked long hours, I had the privilege of employing over 1700 women over a 30-year period in my salon. I worked hard and I made sure my staff did the same. I believed that's what success requires. And it did indeed bring me success, but it also brought exhaustion. At that time, I didn't yet understand that money was energy. I saw it as something I had to chase and have full control of. I didn't realize that the same energy I put into loving my clients, training my staff, building community, and uplifting others was what was truly feeding my prosperity. Over the years, through prayer, meditation, and spiritual study, I came to understand something powerful: Money is not my source, God is.

Money is simply one of the ways God expresses His love and provision in my life. When I started seeing money as a flow instead of a fight, everything changed. I stopped gripping so tightly. I stopped worrying if a major unexpected bill came in. I began to bless my money, literally holding it in my hands and thanking God for it before spending it. I always gave to others joyfully, but back then I didn't understand it for the positive energetic exchange I know it to be now. Generosity keeps energy circulating. And wouldn't you know it , the more grateful and open I became, the more blessings seemed to find me. Unexpected opportunities, new clients, divine connections... everything began to flow naturally, without strain. I realized that abundance responds to appreciation. When you appreciate what you have, you multiply it. When you fear losing it, you block it.

Now, at this stage of my life, I define wealth through a much deeper lens. True wealth is waking up in peace, not in pursuit. It's having the strength to dance in TikTok videos with my kids, its slowing down enough to appreciate and notice beautiful music playing, It's laughing so hard at one of my middle daughter family pranks. It's undergoing major surgery in January 2025 to remove a tumor from my head and healing without a single complication, a living testimony of God's grace.

It's rebuilding a once-broken relationship with my daughter and watching it blossom into love, understanding, and mutual respect. It's having a sound mind, a soft heart, and the freedom to travel this beautiful world with authenticity and purpose.

Wealth, I've come to realize, is not found in what we possess but in how deeply we live, how freely we love, and how connected we remain to the Divine. That is the true abundance, the kind that can never be taken away.

Money is beautiful, but peace is priceless. And when your energy is aligned with love, purpose, and gratitude, you will never lack anything. So bless your money, bless your work, bless your home, and bless the energy that flows through it all.

And remember, **you are already abundant.** You always have been.

When we finally understand that we are energy, we begin to move differently through the world. We become more intentional about what we give our attention to and who we allow into our space. Just as you wouldn't pollute clear water with toxins, you begin to protect your personal energy field from negativity, gossip, and chaos. You start to realize that everything you consume, not just food, but music, conversations, media, and thoughts, either raises or lowers your vibration. Energy hygiene is just as important as physical hygiene. Cleansing your spirit daily through prayer, silence, or even a simple moment of gratitude keeps your frequency pure and high.

The people you surround yourself with also influence your energy field. Spend time with those who uplift you, inspire you, and make you feel safe to be your authentic self. Notice how your body feels around others, do you feel drained or energized? Your body never lies. Energy recognizes energy. The more you align with love, peace, and authenticity, the more you will attract people and experiences that reflect that same vibration. Remember, we don't chase alignment, we *become* it.

Energy is also communication. You don't always have to speak to be understood. Your energy introduces you before you say a word. That's why inner work is so important, it's not just for you, it's for everyone whose life you touch.

When your energy is calm and clear, you become a healing presence. You walk into a room and people can *feel* peace. You may not even realize it, but your vibration has the power to soften hearts, inspire kindness, and remind others of their own light.

As you continue this journey of understanding energy, know this: you are a divine conductor in God's orchestra of life. Every thought you think, every emotion you feel, every word you speak sends out a ripple into the universe. That ripple touches others, shapes outcomes, and creates worlds. This is the power and responsibility of being an energetic being. We are not separate from the Divine, we *are* divine energy in motion, expressing itself in human form. So, live with intention. Protect your peace. Honor your frequency. And remember, energy never lies, and it never dies. It only evolves. You are evolving as well. Every prayer, every breath, every act of love and kindness raises your vibration and brings you closer to the Divine frequency of truth and harmony.

You are not just in the universe, you are part of the very energy that created it. And once you truly embrace that, life will never feel the same again.

As you finish this chapter, I invite you to take a deep breath, in through your nose, out slowly through your mouth, and allow yourself to *feel* the truth of what you've just read. You are not separate from the energy that creates worlds. You are a living, breathing extension of it. Each thought, each emotion, each intention you carry sends a signal into the universe, shaping what you attract and experience. That's why staying centered, grateful, and grounded in peace and love is so powerful. You are not a victim of energy; you are a master of it. You have the power to shift your vibration at any moment, to create peaceful stillness instead of reactive drama, kindness instead of cruelty, love instead of fear, and unencumbered flow instead of resistance.

Let this affirmation be your reminder whenever you feel disconnected, overwhelmed, or uncertain. Speak it aloud. Repeat it again and again until you feel it in your spirit. Allow it to realign you with the divine current that lives within and around you.

✦ I Am Energy

I am divine energy in motion.
Every breath I take connects me to God's infinite flow.
Peace flows through me,
Love radiates from me,
Abundance surrounds me.
I vibrate in harmony
With all that is good, pure, and true.
My energy is sacred,
My spirit is powerful,
My heart is limitless. I am light. I am love.
I am one with the Source of all creation.
And so it is.

Six

Visualize It

Creative visualization has proven to be so beneficial in my life, which is why I want to share this amazing tool with all of you. I have briefly touched on the subject in the previous chapters, but I want to expand further on it here. We have the power to close our eyes and pretend the things we desire actually exist. Pretending that they exist is the secret to actually manifesting them into your life. Children use their imagination to do this all day long. We are born with this natural ability to create things in our mind. Holding thoughts and images in our minds until we feel as if they are real is the key to bringing all the things we want into our lives. The thoughts we focus on are the ones that matter most. We can control our thoughts, which will give us control over our lives.

Russell Simmons' books, *"Super Rich"* and *"Success Through Stillness,"* along with Eckhart Tolle's *"The Power of Now"* were all instrumental in teaching me the importance of sitting still and monitoring my thoughts. *"Super Rich"* in particular left a great impression on me because being the huge business mogul that Russell is, I'm certain many were drawn to the title believing he was giving the world the secrets of how to attain wealth. I remember how intrigued I was to find that the wealth he spoke of in his book was spiritual and emotional wealth, which are vitally important to sustain financial wealth, but Russell Simmons understood, as I do now, that all the money in the universe won't give you peace of mind.

I get excited about the concepts I speak about in my books and I have unshakable faith in them. However there have been many instances in my life where I had to truly work all the tools I believe in, to recenter myself and return to a place of knowing that what I believe in is indeed real. Life has thrown me many "sucker punches," and during these times I had to reevaluate and reaffirm my beliefs.

I became a grandmother for the first time on June 6, 2019. My oldest daughter, Joi, gave birth to a beautiful baby boy, named Raiden Jesse Spears, named after my father, Jesse Paul Fisher who died when I was ten. Although my daughter and I tried our best to arrange things so I would not miss Raiden's birth, the minute I got onto a plane headed to Tampa, Florida for a speakers' training with Delatorro McNeal III called "Crush The Stage," she went into labor. I could not believe it. I was beyond devastated. All of our efforts to ensure that the baby came before or after my trip had failed. I could not believe I was going to miss the birth of my first grandchild. I was absolutely inconsolable on the plane. This was not a moment I would ever get back.

I'm still not sure how I was able to receive the message in flight with my cell phone on airplane mode, but somehow it came through while I was still in the air. I was so hurt that I was going to miss this monumental occasion that I began to cry uncontrollably. I got up from my seat and went to the back where three stewardesses were preparing to serve lunch to the passengers. I walked into the back where they were and I just cried and cried to them, telling them I was not going to be present for the birth of my first grandchild. They were very sweet and understanding. They hugged me and gave me a bottle of wine to calm me and I returned to my seat. I still couldn't stop crying. My distress was so loud and obnoxious that I felt obligated to explain to the man sitting next to me what the problem was. He was kind and he said some comforting words, which I don't remember, and I laid my head on the window and attempted to suffer through the remainder of the flight silently.

Approximately one hour before the plane landed I took out one of my journals and began to write a poem for my new grandson:

Baby Raiden
I have waited for you all week Lil' guy
And as soon as I'm up in the sky
You choose to say "Hi",
I have cried like a baby on this plane
The stewardesses thought I was in physical pain.
I told them I'm missing your birth.
They said, "Don't cry - celebrate his journey to earth."
I told them that this was a special time.
They comforted me and gave me free wine.
Grammie can't wait to meet you.
Your life will be so Amazing!
We all love you so much.
I can't wait to meet you and feel your soft new touch
I'm so sorry I'm on a plane headed to train, in another state.
Trying to make sure that I am Great!
And worthy of the gift of your love.
My precious Grandson, My Lil' Dove.
I will see you soon. I'm filled with Joy.
Welcome to the world Grammie's Baby Boy.

SaBrina Fisher Reece, 6/4/2019

Aside from being absolutely crushed that I missed the birth of my first grandchild, when the plane descended, I felt the most excruciating pain in my ears. I had done a lot of flying over the past four years and never had I experienced anything this uncomfortable. (This was what led to me making an appointment with the ear, nose, and throat specialist, which resulted in the findings mentioned in Chapter 8). The plane landed and I called my daughter from the airport immediately. She was still en route to the hospital to deliver the baby. I sat down inside the airport and she and I cried and cried on the phone like it was the end of the world. We are very close.

I convinced myself that for whatever reason, I was not meant to be there for the delivery. It was the only thought that calmed me. Maybe God didn't feel I would have been able to see her in so much pain. Fortunately, due to modern technology, I was able to view the entire birth via Facetime.

Although I was grateful that I got to see his birth virtually, the stress of the entire situation caused me to be less than prepared for the three-day intensive speakers training that I went to Tampa, Florida to attend. I was distracted, and it took a ton of positive self-talk to get through the training. Each day when I got back to my hotel room, I had to take a moment to close my eyes and visualize myself inside the classroom, speaking confidently on stage. Fortunately, it was a very small class, which made it a lot easier. I learned that at times we may feel we have done all we can to be the best we can, but when we meet others that are better, we realize we need to keep working harder. Our instructor, Delatorro McNeal III, is a world-renowned speaker, and the confidence he exuded onstage was definitely something I wanted for myself. He challenged me in ways that were clearly necessary, but I was intimidated. During my final speech on the third day, he kept stopping me and making me begin again. My ego led me to believe he was picking on me and I began to take it personally. I know better than to take things personally, but in these moments, I could not fight it off. There was a moment where I had a choice: to sit down, get my feelings in check and return to the stage and deliver my speech again, or walk out. Since walking out is not my style and goes against everything I believe in, I sat down and got my nerves together first, then I began to write affirmations on postcards reassuring myself that I could do this.

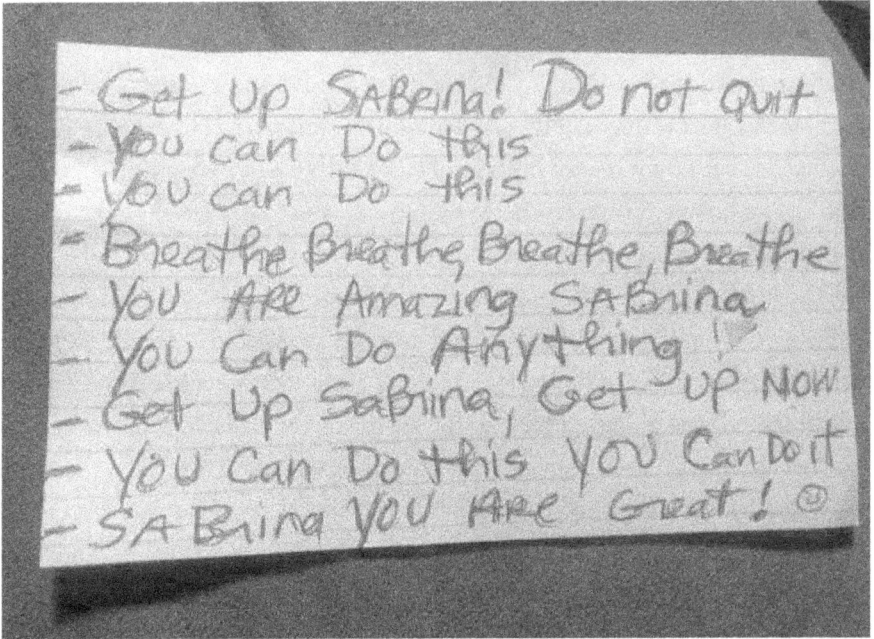

I was scared to death to go back on stage and possibly be stopped mid-speech again, but something inside me knew that if I could get through this, I would be a much better speaker in the end. My heart was pounding. I tried in those few moments to script something, but I knew it was best If I simply spoke from my heart. Other than the instructor and students, several other people had been invited to judge and evaluate our final presentations. That additional pressure definitely didn't make it easier. My old friend, **"Ego"**, crept into my mind while I was waiting to go back up again and tried to convince me that the evaluations from the instructor and the guest were biased. "They didn't like me," is what I attempted to tell myself. I wanted to run with that, but one thing I'm excellent at is recognizing ego. Ego is no friend to us and it will distract us from completing tasks we need to evolve to the next level. I traveled to Tampa for this expert training because after years of studying Delatorro McNeal, I knew he was the best, so I quickly told "ego" to shut up and move the heck on, and I continued to breathe and encourage myself.

I got up after restructuring my speech in only fifteen minutes in my head. My nerves were at an all-time high, but mentally I was determined to incorporate some of the techniques that were given to me after my first evaluation. This was one of the hardest things I have ever done. I had to do a lot of self-talk, but I was there to learn. I had to lay my ego down and become completely humble. I felt attacked. I was very emotional and felt like a failure, however it was all in my mind. Not one of the judges called me a failure or said any of those negative things I was thinking to me. I said them to myself in my mind. I had to work through that, and I had to do it quickly. I wanted to scream, walk out, and give up but I knew I would never forgive myself, nor would I learn the lesson that the universe used this moment to teach me. I took several deep breaths and cast away the negative thoughts. I continued my internal affirmations all the way back to the stage.

Needless to say, I did it! I landed it within the allotted ten minutes given to each student. I delivered a magnificent speech, implementing all of the new tools I just learned which earned me my "Crush The Stage" speaking certificate. It helped me advance greatly as a speaker. I learned so much from that experience. I grew in so many areas. I pushed myself when I truly was so emotional from the initial critique that I wanted to give up. I learned to incorporate techniques into my speech that would allow me to humbly sell my book from the stage as well. Selling from the stage is unquestionably something I had no idea how to do. I had been giving my book away because I wanted others to have the skills I used to feel better in life. Most importantly I tested the very tools I teach to others on myself, and they worked! I needed to encourage myself in that uncomfortable moment and I did. Although I thought I was going to die at the time, I am so glad I stuck it out and I would do it all over again.

When I got back to my hotel room to decompress from it all I was so sincerely proud of myself. I utilized the very tools of affirmations and creative visualization to make myself get back on that stage when every ounce of me wanted to quit. I did not quit, and I left there feeling great. Internal work is not always easy, but the mental battles are the very ones we need to win. Going to full-out war with the internal enemies of ego, self-doubt and fear will prove to be the most significant war you will ever fight. I may have missed the birth of my grandson, but I developed something so wonderful with-in myself that made it all worth it. I returned home the next day to meet my beautiful first grandchild.

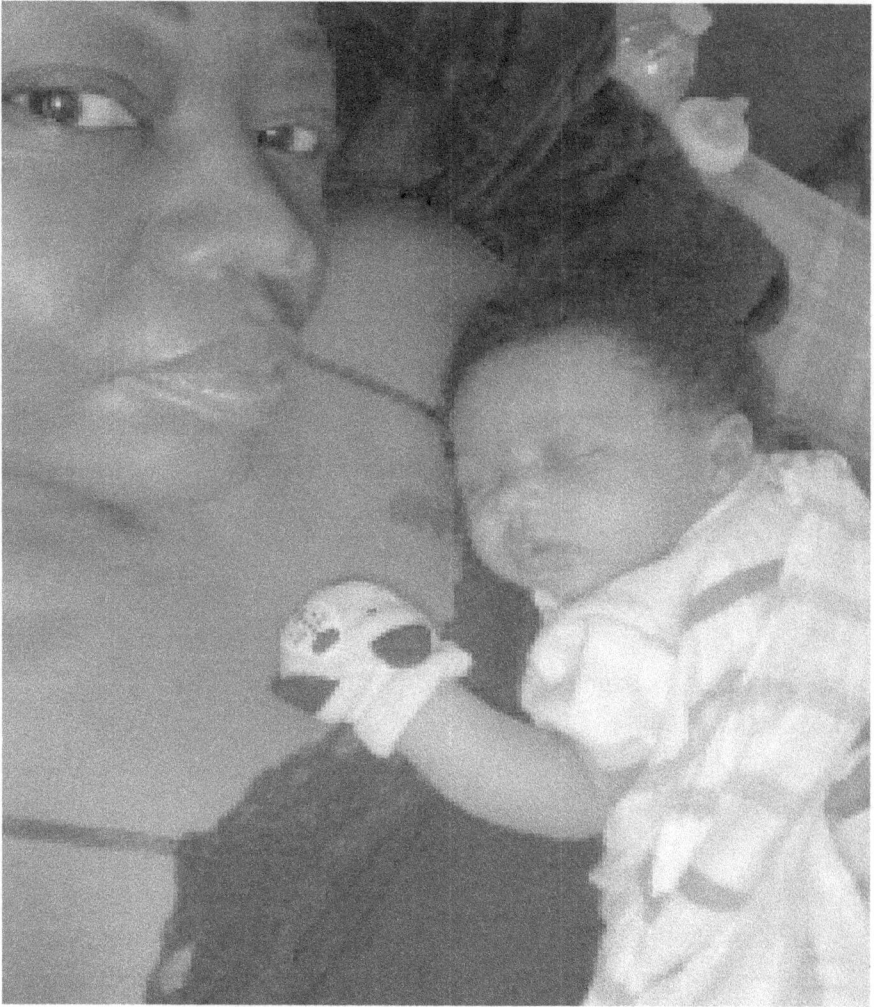

I am so grateful to have lived long enough to see my children's children. There were many times throughout my life that I never thought I would live long enough to see my grandchildren, but once I took control of my life and began to use my natural gift of imagination to create a better life, I became excited about living. I became even more excited about creating a great life. I no longer believe that I was doomed to suffer throughout this life experience as I once did. I began working on changing the narrative in my head. I wanted to live a long healthy life, but I knew I had to mentally create that reality. I had to reprogram all of the images of death. I would practice seeing myself at a much older age. I would create images of having conversations with my great-grandchildren, embracing and encouraging them in full mind, body, and soul. We don't just want to live a long life, we must do the mental work to ensure a long, *healthy* life, free of sickness and disease. No one is meant to simply suffer through life. We are all meant to be happy. Happiness begins inside first. Imagine that you are happy, healthy and prosperous and before you know it you will be.

Training your imagination is not easy, start with simple exercises. Imagine yourself five years from now walking into the home you desire to live in. Imagine the car you want to drive. Imagine the beautiful grass and flowers outside of your new home. If you have a fear of death, imagine yourself at a much later stage in life signifying that you will live a long life. When I get fearful of death, I imagine myself at my eighty-fifth birthday party. I imagine myself smiling and dancing and basking in the joy of being surrounded by all of my children, grandchildren and great-grandchildren. I make sure to be specific in the visual by seeing myself strong and healthy enjoying my birthday. That part is very important. We must be detailed when we do our visualization techniques. You wouldn't want to create a scene where you live to be one hundred but you are sick,disabled, and unhealthy would you? Make sure you visualize yourself happy and healthy. God gave us the power to think anything we desire into existence. This power is active even when we are not aware of it. That is why monitoring our thoughts is necessary.

I have owned several businesses, some of which I knew nothing about before opening. Inked 4 Life Tattoo Studio is proof that you can precisely design something completely in your mind before it exists in the real world. I initially took possession of a commercial building because I created a barber shop for my son Justin who was in barber school. I named that salon, "Just-In-Time Barber and Beauty Salon." After spending an enormous amount of time and money putting this business together it became apparent that my son did not want the responsibility of being a business owner. He said he wanted to become a rapper, which was the dream of so many young African American boys at the time. I always told him that he did not have to continue this as a lifelong career, but it would give him a source of income until he figured out exactly what he wanted to be.

Justin was quite strong-willed, and I was stuck with a barber shop that I had no desire or time to run. I always let my son know that he did not have to make a career out of the barber shop. It was simply my gift to him to generate an income until he was able to pursue his dreams. However he was still quite disinterested in running it. My primary business, Braids By SaBrina, was located two doors down, and it consumed the majority of my time and energy. However, I was locked into a lease for a few years, so I needed to do something with the building. I drove around and scanned the neighborhood for ideas of what I could transform the barber-shop into. I came up with the idea of a tattoo shop. Tattooing was quite popular and there was no direct competitor anywhere near.I knew nothing of how to run this particular type of business. My only experience with tattoo shops was when I had gone to one to receive a tattoo. However, in my mind I began to create the business. This was at a time in my life where I had no idea the importance of creative visualization. I had not yet learned these mental tools, but by default I designed this business in my mind from beginning to end. It had beautiful, fluorescent green lettering to catch the attention of those in oncoming traffic. Fortunately, I was able to utilize most of the furniture from the barber shop. I did a lot of the artwork on the wall myself. I even drew a large koi fish on the floor. It was a fun and exciting new experience.

In my sleep, I would come up with ideas and then get up and implement them the next day. I repeat I had no experience whatsoever in the tattoo industry. I went around town and visited other tattoo parlors to get an idea of the basic setup. Thirty days later I opened the doors to Inked 4 Life Tattoo

Studio on Adams Blvd. A full- fledged business that began as a simple thought.

Our minds are so amazing. The mind is indeed magical. Even before I knew how to use visualization techniques as a tool, I was successful in using them by default. When I think back on how I used my mind to create that business, I get inspired. I never allowed fear or doubt to enter my mind. I never once remember thinking that it was not possible to own a tattoo shop. I visualized it and voila! I became the sole proprietor of yet another successful business. That opportunity exists for everyone. Thinking back on that reminds me that we can do absolutely anything as long as we ignore those little voices in our heads that tell us we cannot.

We are creators and anything we truly desire we can have. I believe this should be taught in kindergarten. Children should learn, as early as possible of the power they possess over their own lives. They should be taught that their lives are like a coloring book and only they possess the crayons. I believe that mankind can indeed evolve, but it starts with each and every individual person recognizing their own greatness. We all must come to terms with the fact that we are not limited unless we choose to be. We can become anyone we chose to become. The possibilities are limitless. We can acquire any level of success we choose. We simply have to train our minds to believe that all things are possible.

Seven

All Things Are Possible

All things are possible, and I know it's hard for us to believe that at times, especially when everything in our lives seems to be going wrong and all of what we desire hasn't shown up. Times when that home loan was denied, or our relationship seems to be falling apart. Maybe we have lost our job, or our car has been repossessed. It seems that none of our prayers have been answered. These are the times when it's hardest to believe that all things are possible, but they are.

It is during these times when we feel defeated that we allow our vibration to become low. We are all energy and we are all vibrating. We appear to be solid, as do the chair we sit in or the car we drive, but everything is vibrating. You can't see it, but you are vibrating at this very moment. What most don't know is that they can change the frequency of their personal vibration. We can choose to vibrate at a higher frequency. It seems natural that during the hardest times of our lives, when tragedy strikes us or our families, or when finances are low and no ends seem to meet, that we feel stressed and afraid. Acknowledge those feelings, but don't stay there. No matter what you are going through, you still have to encourage yourself and raise your vibration.

I became inspired once I realized that I could change the way I felt. I never had to accept being in a bad mood, no matter what I believed the cause of it to be. If by chance I woke up feeling down, learning that I did not have to accept those feelings and carry them throughout my day was very helpful. We all have the opportunity to reject negative feelings as soon as we recognize them and use whichever tool we find effective in making ourselves instantly feel better. Gospel music or listening to 432 hz binaural beats works well for me. The gospel music instantly makes me happy and grateful. The pure tone version of the 432 hz binaural beats helps me to concentrate,especially when writing. Find what works for you and don't hesitate to use it center yourself and to uplift your mood.

A quick way for me to pull myself out of a negative space is to write down and acknowledge the things I have to be grateful for. We all have many things to be grateful for. If you are having money problems, but you still have a job, then you have something to be grateful for. If your car isn't running at its best but it's still running and getting you to that job everyday, then you have something to be grateful for. If you are employed, allow yourself to feel gratitude for having a job when many do not. Simply taking a moment to sit with and bask in those feelings of gratitude will instantly encourage you. Feeling encouraged motivates us to accomplish more in life.

It is imperative that we realize it takes a conscious effort to make positive change on a subconscious level. If we want a better, more productive life, especially internally, then we must take external steps towards securing our internal happiness. We must come to understand that the internal is just as important or even more important than the external. We must work daily on the subjective aspect of happiness in order to reap the objective benefits of a great life. Subjective things are things you cannot see, feel or touch. Objective things are tangible, things we can touch and see. If we master subjective/internal happiness, objective/external happiness is soon to follow.

Like attracts like. Positive attracts positive and negative attracts negative. It is an immutable universal law. Just like gravity and karma. No matter what you do or who you are if you jump off the roof of a building you will go down. The results of karma are not as visible, but they are unchangeable as well. Kindness returns unto you kindness, hate returns hate it's unavoidable. Universal laws are laws that are inflexible and not subject to change. They are the laws of God.

The Law of Attraction is definitely something you should familiarize yourself with. You attract back to you exactly the energy and vibration that you put out into the world. If you get up in the morning and you aren't feeling your best, take a few minutes before you get up to raise your vibration. Intentionally uplift the way you feel inside so the energy you release into the world is positive. Don't allow yourself to stay in a bad mood or stay sad, unhappy, or disappointed. Low energy attracts more low energy. High energy does the same. We can't afford to proceed with the tasks of our day without elevating our energetic frequency. If you want to have a great day, take a few moments and first speak that intent into the universe. Actually, say the words "Today will be a great day." Better yet, say, "Today Is a great day." Speak of it as a fact and not a wish. Repeat that while you brush your teeth and do your other morning rituals. What most people aren't aware of is that words and thoughts have an energetic frequency too. When you speak negatively, saying things such as, "I'm broke," "I'm dumb," or "I will never get ahead in life," you project that negativity into the world. What you send out comes back. Let's work on making sure the things that come back are good and positive.

We are subconsciously programmed to instantly put up barriers to impede our own thoughts of greatness and success. Try to monitor your thoughts enough to catch yourself the next time it happens. Eventually it will become a positive habit that will change your life.

I used to say to myself, "I want to own a laundromat," but no sooner than the thought came into my mind, I would have thoughts which said, "No, that's too much work," or "Where would you find all those washing machines? You know nothing about this type of business SaBrina." These are self-sabotaging thoughts. This is an example of how we talk ourselves out of greatness. These are the barriers I am speaking of. We create these untruths in our minds. It is for us to simply plant the seed in the garden and allow it to grow. Plant a positive seed not a negative one. We need not concern ourselves with the particulars of how it will be manifested, we just need to believe wholeheartedly that it will. We absolutely must "believe in things unseen as if they already are"

"Now Faith is the substance of things hoped for, the evidence of things unseen."
(Hebrew 11:1)

This may not always be the easiest thing to do, but it's the key to being able to manifest your heart's desires into your life. Pretend! Pretend as a child would. Pretend you have that home you want; pretend you have already opened that business you have been dreaming about. Commit an extensive amount of time thinking about it. Literally close your eyes and see the big "Grand Opening" sign in your mind. Design the lettering and the colors. Visualize the people coming in the front door with big smiles congratulating you on the opening day of your business. Force yourself to smile and allow yourself to fill up inside with pride for your accomplishment. Stick with that visual long enough to actually feel the corresponding emotion at that moment. Keep the images in your head until you can connect emotions with them as well. The visual Image plus emotion is key. You'll know it's working when you find yourself smiling externally and internally.

I can always tell when I am following my destined path. People will show up in my life and strike up a conversation that mirrors my own concepts and beliefs. This positive thinking ideology is not always well-received. Many times, I am hesitant to bring up the way I think to others. Even as I type this, I know that despite a huge percentage of the world not being open enough to hear and accept that we are in control of our destiny, and that our thoughts and feelings shape that very destiny, I know that my purpose here on this earth is to continue to deliver that message. Part of my mission here on Earth is to teach people the tools I used to transform my mindset, which ultimately transformed my entire life.

When I come across an author, thought, leader, or speaker who seems to be on the same path I'm on, it makes me emotional. Positive emotions flood through me because even if those people never know I read their book, or watched their videos, my life was impacted by their work because they followed their purpose. My goal is to do the same for others with my literary work. My books and speeches will impact lives. That is what motivates me to continue. The fact that others will learn to love themselves and live their lives to the fullest makes it all worth it.

All things are possible. See yourself in your mind's eye exactly as the person you want to be. You can be anyone you truly want to be. In no way am I insinuating that developing intentional positive pictures in your head is easy. It takes work and a lot of practice. However, this will be the best skill you've ever learned. Mastering this skill will allow you to take part in all the wonderful things this world has to offer.

The practice of creative visualization will get easier and easier. You can hone this skill by attempting to visualize small things like a banana. Close your eyes and tell your mind you see a banana, then switch it to an apple. Learning to creatively visualize takes practice. The images may seem fuzzy or unclear at first. As you continue to do it you will see how quickly the images you call upon appear faster and faster the more you practice this technique. Eventually the images will be clear and solid. You will see how the mind creates pictures instantly as soon as we think of them. That's how God and the universe work. Plant the image with your thoughts and let God do the rest. Remember mastering this ability takes focused intentional time and practice just like any other skill. Please don't get frustrated and quit. Sticking with this will change your life as it did mine. This is the amazing magic of your mind.

We no longer have to live in a world where we have to sacrifice some of our desire for others. Everything is a possibility; we simply have to learn how to bring them to us. We don't have to give up on wealth to have happiness, or sacrifice the desire for peace in order to be successful. We can have it all.

I don't know anyone who does not want more of something in life, be it peace of mind, abundant wealth, or happiness. Everyone has hopes and dreams of something more. This book will reinforce the fact that you can indeed have exactly what you want and plenty of it. However, many people are unsure of exactly what they desire. What do you want? What will make you happy? Sit down and clarify in detail precisely what you believe needs to be added to your life to make you pleased and content. Our thoughts escape us at times. We will think or dream of something and after proceeding with our daily activities we will forget. I suggest always keeping a journal with you to jot down your thoughts, goals and ideas as quickly as your mind delivers them to you. Many of those ideas will prove to be quite valuable. Later, you can pick one at a time and visualize having it. Give each thing you list in your journal its own individual creative visualization time. Practice this positive tool daily and soon it will astonish you how fast all of the wonderful things show up in your life.

Remember, all things are possible; not some, but all. I repeat that continuously because I want you to know that there is no goal that is too big. *It's all possible!* Accepting that is one of the first steps in changing your life through positive thinking. There are no limits other than the ones we accept in our mind. We must learn how to maintain a positive state of mind, because doing so will drastically change the things that show up in our lives. Remember that the mind is our own personal garden. It accepts exactly what we plant. It's our genie in a bottle. The mind will grant our true wishes, good or bad. We must understand that. The mind won't say, "No, I don't think that is a good idea." If you plant it, it will grow!

Everything you desire is possible, bad things included. We must not focus on bad thoughts. We have the ability to manifest undesirable things into our lives also. Things that are not in our best interest or in line with God's plan for us are also possible. *All* things are possible, so we must guide our thoughts toward the possibilities we sincerely want in our lives.

Do not waste time thinking and fearing that you will have a car accident, or you will. Do not focus your mind power on your fears of divorce or that is the very thing that will happen to your marriage. The thoughts we allow our minds to concentrate on will show up in our actual lives. Many of us do not realize how much time we spend thinking of the things we fear.

What you fear will appear! You can be certain of that. Take time to identify what those fears are so you can recognize them when they show up in your mind and quickly eliminate them.

Once we fully understand that anything we apply focused thought to can and will appear in our lives, then we should not continue to resist the fact that it's necessary to learn to focus on the good and positive, and cast out all other thoughts before they materialize. Many of the things present in my life today, I have to admit, I committed a significant amount of time thinking of them. Good or bad, the rules are the same. Catch yourself the next time you find yourself daydreaming. It may seem harmless, but once you stop yourself and immediately reflect back to what you were just daydreaming about, you may find it was not positive. If that is the case, then you will see why this practice is necessary. Catch those negative, fearful thoughts immediately and switch them into positive ones.

The Bible states in Matthew 19:26, *"But Jesus Beheld them and said unto them, "With men this is impossible, but with God all things are possible"* or in Luke 1:37 *"For with God nothing shall be impossible."* Growing up in the Christian church I have heard many different versions of these scriptures combined with their many different interpretations. I believe that from the beginning of time God created us with no limitations. We have always been capable of great, amazing things but somehow we lost our way. At some point in our existence humans seemed to accept restrictions on our lives that were never meant to exist, restrictions that technically do not exist until we convince ourselves that they do. This has been the downfall of mankind. This is why everyone is not a successful inventor, adding their life-changing contributions to the world. We all are capable of great ideas. We are all great. That amazing inspiration for creation is inside of us all. We just need to remember that it's there.

Watching inspirational movies of people who persevered despite great odds and accomplished their dreams are great reminders that we can do anything. Stories such as that of Bart Millard, the lead singer of the group, Mercy Me, have uplifted me. His life story inspired the world in the movie and hit song, "I Can Only Imagine." I've watched this movie at least a dozen times. The feelings of hope that you feel when you watch others strive for success and win are priceless. This is often the push we need to keep going until we accomplish our goals. Knowing that all of our goals are attainable should keep that fire burning in all of us.

Another story that inspired me was the story of Tommy Caldwell and Kevin Jorgeson. They were rock climbers determined to conquer a massive mountain in El Capitan called, "The Dawn Wall." When I began watching the documentary my first thought was, *Why would anyone want to do this?* Once I finished the show, I realized it does not matter if others understand the "why" as long as we do. Whatever stirs up that drive and gives us the will power needed to recognize that we can do anything is all that matters. For some, it may be climbing the highest mountain. For others, it may be running for president or becoming a best-selling author. Many may have dreams of acting on the big screen or becoming a great singer. Whatever it is that motivates us as humans to keep going, that is what we all need to hold on to.

All goals are attainable. There is no goal you can set for yourself that is too big to accomplish. Do not allow anyone to convince you of that. More importantly, do not convince yourself that certain goals are unattainable. Nothing you desire is insurmountable. If you are willing to commit to the work needed to bring your desires into your reality, then nothing can stop you from achieving them. Yes, the physical work, the hustle and bustle are important, but the most important work is the mental work; learning to keep your thoughts positive. Believe that what you want is already done, not "will be," not "one day," but already done. Close your eyes and feel the feelings of already having what you desire. And like magic you will reap the objective benefits of having it. There is nothing that is impossible. Get a pen and paper, write down your clearly defined goals and get to work.

Abundance is a concept that I speak about regularly. I have several Youtube videos entitled **Abundance Is Real**. I am very passionate about the fact that I believe all people can experience abundance in all areas of their lives. Financial abundance is something people feel that they have to sacrifice in exchange for good health, happiness, and peace. We do not have to forgo wealth. We can have financial abundance too.

Yes, working hard is half the battle, but I am of the mindset that prosperity begins first in the mind. **Your Mind is Magic,** and our minds are the magic wand that will allow financial wealth to show up in our lives. The action of work is secondary. One can work all day and night but if he doesn't believe that he deserves abundance he won't have it.

There is a scripture in the bible that says, *"For whoever has, he shall be given more, and they will have abundance. Whoever does not have, even what they have will be taken from them".* Matthew 13:12

I think many people misinterpret this scripture as God being cruel. That's not it at all. Since poverty is a mindset, God is simply saying for those who believe they deserve wealth will receive more, but for those who gain some degree of financial freedom, but are still of the mindset that they don't deserve it, they will eventually lose it. They will lose it not because they don't deserve it, but because they don't believe that they deserve it. They are surprised by the prosperity, so they expect to lose it. We must train our minds to expect wealth.

Have you ever noticed how some big business tycoons lose everything and go bankrupt, yet somehow rebuild everything in a short amount of time? The only thing they possess that differs from many others is the expectation of success. They see themselves as nothing but wealthy even when their business has failed. Poverty is a mindset that can be changed. No one has to settle for poverty. The first steps in changing it begins in the mind.

Each one of us is entitled to the riches of the world, but we cannot experience that wealth in its entirety until we rid our minds of a poverty mindset. Understandably, after years of expecting financial hardship it can take a lot of consistent work to reverse those habits. Begin with a simple daily affirmation:

"I am rich in all areas of my life, money flows frequently
and effortlessly into my life."

Abundance is real and something we all can enjoy. Make a decision that no matter what your current financial situation, you will begin to thank God daily for abundance. Even if your mind is trying to convince you that you are being dishonest, keep putting thoughts of gratitude out into the universe. Keep telling God, "Thank you," for the wealth he has blessed you with. Act as if you are the wealthiest person in the world. Mentally declare prosperity for yourself and believe me it will appear. Do not try to concern yourself with how and where it will come from. Just believe that is possible and already done.

Eight

Master Your Mind

⚜

Proverbs 23:7 "For as he thinketh in his heart, so is he."

Our thoughts are far more than fleeting mental activity, they are living energy. Every thought carries a vibration, a signal sent out into the universe that attracts experiences matching its frequency. Every word we speak, every mental image we hold, communicates with the unseen realm of creation. We are immersed in a vibrational universe: nothing is still, nothing is neutral. Every object, sound, emotion, and thought emits frequency. When we dwell on fear, anger, limitation, or resentment, we send out a signal that draws back more of the same. Just like a boomerang, what you send out returns exactly that to you. Conversely, when we focus on love, gratitude, joy, and faith, the universe responds in harmony, flow, and divine alignment.

The good news is this: we hold the power to choose. Every morning, we decide how we will begin our vibrational day. Will we rise heavy with worry, lack, and self-judgment, or will we awaken in gratitude, faith, and love? When we choose gratitude first, thanking God before anything else, we tune our internal frequency to abundance. That frequency begins to draw more of what we appreciate.

I personally program my subconscious to thank God immediately upon waking. Gratitude is more than a habit; it is a spiritual lever that opens doors and aligns us with divine flow. Choosing to begin the day in gratitude is the first conscious act of thought mastery, a declaration that we are co-creators with God.

God gave us the power to think, imagine, and believe because we are made in His image. Just as God creates, so too are we designed to create. Every invention, every song, every business, Beautiful art piece, every breakthrough first began as a single thought in someone's mind. Thought is the blueprint, and emotion is the divine energy that breathes life into that design.

Throughout my life, I have owned and operated several businesses, but there is one that will forever stand as a personal testimony of how creation begins in the mind. It was long before I had ever heard the phrase "creative visualization." Back then, I didn't know that what I was doing was spiritual law in motion. I knew nothing about manifestation, so wasn't intentionally trying to manifest anything; I was simply *consumed* by the vision. My heart, my thoughts, my energy were all wrapped around bringing that dream to life. I thought about it constantly. I visualized every detail. I could see the colors, the design, the name, and the feeling of the space before a single door had opened.

That dream became *Inked 4 Life Tattoo Studio*, located on Adams Blvd, right next to my braiding salon. You can still find videos of it on YouTube today. I occupied three commercial building on Adams Blvd. at the same time. *Braids By SaBrina Braiding Shop, Inked 4 Life Tattoo Studio* and *The Braids By SaBrina Braiding School*. Looking back, I realize I had manifested those businesses through the divine creative process by holding the images so clearly in my heart and mind that the universe had no choice but to make it real. God had no choice but to grant me the desires of my heart. That holds true for us all.

This experience taught me something sacred: creation doesn't always come from effort alone it comes from alignment. Even without knowing the spiritual laws, I was living them. I was focused, inspired, and emotionally invested. I believed, even without realizing it, belief was the very key that unlocked the manifestation. I believed strongly and without doubt that each business would come into fruition.

So, if we can manifest by accident, through focus and emotion alone, imagine what we can create once we awaken to the truth of who we really are and intentionally partner with the divine power within us. We are co-creators with God. Our thoughts are prayers in motion, and every vision held in faith is an invitation for Heaven to work through us.

✦ **Buddha** said, "What you think, you become. What you feel, you attract. What you imagine, you create."
  ✦ **Confucius** is believed to have expressed a similar sentiment in ancient Chinese philosophy about mindset shaping reality.
  ✦ **Henry Ford** rephrased it famously in the early 1900s: *"Whether you think you can, or you think you can't — you're right."*
  ✦**Ralph Waldo Emerson said,** *"We become what we think about all day long."*

When you imagine something with feeling, when you see it vividly in your mind and feel it in your heart ,you are engaging the spiritual laws of manifestation. You are not daydreaming; you are building in the invisible realm. The unseen always precedes the seen. Faith is the bridge carrying imagination from thought to form. Emotion, energy in motion, fuels creation. A thought without feeling is like a car without gas, it may look good but won't move anywhere.

This is why gratitude, love, and joy are such powerful attractors, they are high-frequency emotions that magnetize more of the same energy back to you. When your thoughts are rooted in these vibrations, life responds in kind. On the contrary, when your thoughts are laced with resentment, worry, or fear, you create energetic resistance, blocking the natural flow of good.

Awareness is always the first step toward transformation. Begin by dedicating just five minutes twice a day to intentionally create positive images in your mind. With each practice, your vision will grow clearer and more vivid. Once the picture is strong in your imagination, add emotion to it, *that's the spark that brings it to life.* Feel what it would feel like if it were already happening. Allow joy, gratitude, and excitement to rise within you as if it's already done.

This is the secret recipe for manifestation, conscious, intentional thought combined with authentic emotion. When thought and feeling unite, they speak the language of the Divine, and creation begins to move in your favor.

Your energy is always sending a message to the universe. Every belief you hold, every feeling you nurture, every word you speak vibrates at a frequency that attracts its equal. If your thoughts are filled with fear or limitation, life will echo that back to you. But when your thoughts align with faith, love, and confidence, you begin to notice that doors open, people appear, and opportunities flow to you effortlessly. Nothing in your outer world can change until you shift what you are vibrating within.

The mind is the architect, but the heart is the builder. Belief bridges the two. Belief gives your vision structure; emotion gives it life. When you believe with your whole being, not just in your head, but in your spirit, the energy of that belief begins to rearrange circumstances on your behalf. That's why Jesus said, *"According to your faith, be it unto you."* It's a reminder that strong belief, faith and feeling are the engines of creation.

So, when you visualize your desires, don't just *see* them, *feel* them. Feel the peace, the gratitude, the joy of already living the life you're creating. As you do, your vibration rises to meet the frequency of that vision. And once you match the vibration of what you desire, the universe has no choice but to deliver it to you.

Divine Law and the Creative Process

The universe operates according to divine laws, eternal principles responding to vibration, not words alone.

✦**Law of Vibration:** Everything moves; nothing rests. Every atom hums with energy.

✦**Law of Attraction:** Like attracts like — not by chance, but by resonance.

✦**Law of Cause and Effect:** Every action has a reaction; every thought has a consequence.

Your dominant thoughts and emotions set your vibration, and your vibration determines what you attract. The mind is like a radio transmitter: you cannot tune into jazz and hear gospel music. Vibrating with lack cannot yield abundance; vibrating with anger cannot produce peace. Align your inner frequency with the life you desire. Jesus said, "Believe that ye receive, and ye shall have." Belief is not just a mental exercise; it is a vibrational knowing that something is already yours in spirit, before it appears in form.

I remember visualizing my beautiful four-bedroom, three-bathroom "forever home" in New Mexico long before I ever stepped foot inside it. In my mind's eye, I could see myself sitting on the balcony off my spacious primary suite, gazing out at the breathtaking Sandia Mountains beneath a pink and purple sky. I imagined the warmth of my daughter beside me as we cooked together in our elegant kitchen, white cabinetry, black and gold accents, sunlight pouring through wide windows.

I pictured my large foyer and the library I designed to hold my beloved vintage book collection, the vaulted ceilings, and the cozy loft space where my kids' computer desks sat beside my sound healing equipment. I saw us working out in the three-car garage, one section transformed into a home gym. I envisioned us planting our feet and grounding in the lush, fertile grass in the large backyard, a space big enough for my garden and an above-ground pool for my children to play and laugh in under the New Mexico sun.

I designed it all first in my imagination, down to the smallest details, and eventually, that vision became my reality. That's the power of creation through thought, emotion, and belief. You have that same power, too, to design, visualize, and attract the life that feels aligned with your soul. Everything begins in the mind. When you hold the image and infuse it with gratitude and joy, life will rise to meet your vision.

Every creation begins as energy, a thought, a feeling, a vision that vibrates before it materializes. The moment you imagine something with love, gratitude, and certainty, you send a powerful signal into the universe. That signal becomes a magnet for experiences, people, and opportunities that match your vibration. Your imagination is not wishful thinking; it's a sacred blueprint. When thought, emotion, and belief unite, the unseen begins to take form. And soon, what once lived only in your mind stands before you as living proof that energy, when aligned with faith and feeling, become reality.

✦ **The Role of Imagination** Imagination is one of God's greatest gifts, divine architecture in motion, not mere child's play. It is the sacred blueprint through which faith paints the vision and emotion breathes life into it. Neville Goddard called imagination "the gateway to reality," reminding us that every creation begins first in the unseen.

Children understand this instinctively. They imagine without fear, limitation, or logic, creating entire worlds from the power of their belief. Yet as adults, we often "unlearn" this divine ability, replacing wonder with reason and faith with doubt. Society teaches us to be practical, to believe only in what we can see, but the spirit knows better.

To manifest fully, we must return to that childlike state of trust and remembrance, to the knowing that imagination is God's language within us. When we dare to dream with conviction, we awaken the creative power already placed in our hands.

But divine creation isn't tested in meditation or theory, it's tested in the chaos of daily life. Traffic, tempers, and triggers are where thought mastery really takes shape. When someone cuts you off on the road, you're given a spiritual choice: you can hand over your peace, or you can choose a higher vibration.

I'll admit, *traffic trauma* is still one of my toughest lessons. Something about those near-miss moments on the freeway instantly stirs a wave of fear and frustration. Before I know it, words I don't normally use start flying out of my mouth! It's not that I'm trying to curse; it's that I momentarily feel my safety, and my children's, has been threatened. That flash of fear transforms into anger, and anger becomes sound. But even in those moments, I'm learning. Awareness is progress.

I've started to pause, take a breath, and remind myself: "God, protect my peace." Because each moment of restraint, patience, and love, even behind the wheel, is a conscious act of co-creation with the Divine.

Anger, frustration, or offense tempt us to react in low vibration. Every time we respond in anger, hostility, or judgment, we hand over our peace to the very energy that hurt us. Reacting may temporarily satisfy the ego, but it disconnects us from divine alignment. Yes, God still loves us, but we cannot live in peace and harmony while out of alignment with His flow.

By the time I was fifty-six, I had come to appreciate and relish my peaceful life. I loved it. It may seem simple to some, but I was genuinely happy and content. Fortunately, my middle daughter, only twenty-three at the time, also cherished our peaceful, simple life. We laughed often, read books, and took evening walks with our dog, Keiko Barkley. We cheered at my youngest daughter's volleyball games and admired the sunsets and the ever-changing clouds. It was a beautiful life for which we were deeply grateful.

That peace didn't come overnight; it was the result of years of inner work, catching my thoughts before they spiraled, choosing calm when chaos called, and learning to breathe through irritation and impatience instead of reacting to it. Peace is earned through spiritual practice. It's built moment by moment, in the quiet choices we make when no one else is watching, in the moments we decide not to argue, not to complain, not to relive the past or predict the worst.

Every choice to stay centered adds another layer of strength to our spiritual foundation. I realized that divine creation isn't about escaping the world; it's about transforming how we move through it. The real test of mastery comes when life feels messy, when tempers flare, plans fall apart, or people disappoint us. That's where spirit is refined.

It's easy to feel evolved in stillness, but true peace is proven when the world gives you a reason to lose it, and you don't. In those moments, when we feel the pull toward anger or frustration, we can pause and remind ourselves, "I am not this emotion. I am the observer of it." That awareness is power. It reconnects us with God in an instant.

When you take a deep breath and whisper, "Peace, be still," not only does the world quiet, the storm within you does too. Each time we choose calm over chaos, grace over grievance, we rise higher in vibration and closer to divine alignment.

The peace I enjoy with my daughters isn't just circumstantial, it is sacred. It is the manifestation of years of intention, forgiveness, and surrender. It is the harvest of choosing love over fear, of practicing gratitude even when life isn't perfect. I learned that joy doesn't come from having everything you want, it comes from wanting and being grateful for everything you already have.

Our walks with Keiko Barkley are more than just strolls around the block; they are meditations in motion. We talk about life, about dreams, about how blessed we are to live in a home filled with laughter, faith, and gentleness. We talk about how grateful we are to have such a magnificent mother,daughter relationship. We notice the smallest miracles, the beautiful trees, the squirrels and birds, the intricacy of the beautiful sky. Those simple moments are proof that peace isn't found in the absence of noise, but in the presence of awareness.

Divine creation is not reserved for grand miracles or supernatural moments. It's found in the quiet choices, when you choose love instead of anger, gratitude instead of complaint, peace instead of reaction. That is the real spiritual work: bringing heaven into the ordinary and finding God not just in prayer, but in the parking lot, the kitchen, the car ride, and the laughter shared at sunset.

Because when your mind is at peace, your world reflects it. And that's when life, simple, beautiful, and divinely aligned, becomes the highest creation of all.

True mastery comes in choosing the high road. Smile instead of curse. Breathe instead of shout. Respond with grace rather than retaliation. These choices do not dismiss God; they honor Him, because they recognize the divine power within you to guide your own vibration.

The same applies to our inner dialogue. Calling yourself "stupid," "unworthy," or "a failure" programs your subconscious to believe it. Speaking to yourself with love, even after mistakes, lifts your vibration toward divine alignment.

Your peace is power. Thoughts shape reality. Every moment is a chance to create anew, to speak life, gratitude, and love, rather than fear and disaster. Mastery is awareness, taking charge of your own life is awareness: catching yourself mid-thought and choosing differently is the ultimate awareness. Over time, your external world reflects your inner discipline. Doors open, relationships heal, ideas flow, and life unfolds in harmony.

Of course, there are times when our faith is tested. Times when circumstances seem impossible. When bills pile up, relationships falter, or dreams feel delayed, that's when you must consciously choose the vibration of possibility. All things are possible, so faith isn't wishful thinking, it's spiritual technology. It's the invisible power that bridges the gap between what is and what can be. Belief in the unseen is what activates manifestation.

But remember: what you plant in the garden of your mind will grow, whether it's faith or fear, abundance or lack. So take a moment to sit quietly with yourself and ask, *What do I truly believe?* If you believe in poverty, struggle, and sickness, those seeds will take root and shape your reality. But if you believe in abundance, happiness, and divine health, that is what will bloom in your life. Define your beliefs clearly, because whatever you hold in faith, the universe will water.

✦ **Hebrews 11:1:** "Now faith is the substance of things hoped for, the evidence of
things unseen."

Faith carries thought from possibility to reality. Prayer, visualization, and words of faith are energetic blueprints. Each thought, word, and feeling is a brick in the invisible foundation.

The universe is not withholding blessings; it is responding to your alignment. Vibrate in fear, and fear meets you. Vibrate in confidence, and confidence returns. Like attracts like by law, not chance. Consistency is key: affirm abundance and cultivate it throughout the day. Live your life on a higher vibration and you will enjoy all that this magnificent world has to offer.

I can't reiterate enough, visualization is sacred. Images in the mind are blueprints for creation. Close your eyes and see the life you desire: your home, career, relationships, peace, joy. Allow feeling to fill every cell of your body. Emotion fuels manifestation. Faith sees it before it appears. Fear works in reverse; energy given to fear could have built your dreams.

When low energy arises, tools like gospel music, sound bowls, prayer, meditation, and vibrational frequencies (528 or 432 Hz) can elevate you. They quiet the mind, realign the spirit, and amplify gratitude. Mastery is not absence of emotion; it is the ability to guide emotion into alignment with love.

Gratitude bridges where you are with where you want to be. Visualize abundance, thank God for blessings, imagine opportunities flowing. Energy shifting; doors opening. Your inner programming can be rewritten. Thoughts that contradict dreams, "I can't," "I'll fail," must be gently redirected with compassion.

Affirmations imprint the subconscious. Faith is certainty in the unseen. The combination of thought, emotion, and belief activates creation.

✦ Practical Daily Practices for Thought Mastery

1. **Morning Gratitude Ritual:** Upon waking, speak three things you are thankful for. Let this set the vibrational tone.
2. **Midday Alignment Check:** Pause, breathe, and notice your thoughts. Shift any low-vibration thinking to a higher thought.
3. **Visualization Exercise:** Close your eyes and picture your desired life in detail, feeling it as real.
4. **Evening Reflection:** Journal your thoughts, affirm lessons learned, and

express gratitude.

5. **Affirmations:** Repeat empowering affirmations, such as: "I am aligned with divine flow. I am co-creating my highest good."

✦ Affirmation of Thought Mastery

My thoughts are sacred energy, aligned with divine creation. I think with intention, speak with faith, and believe with love. I am the master of my mind, the designer of my reality, and the co-creator of my destiny. All things are possible because I am one with the infinite mind of God. My thoughts are divine vibrations of creation. I think with faith, feel with love, and align my heart with God's truth. I am a co-creator with the Universe, manifesting joy, peace, and abundance in every area of my life."

Nine

Our Subconscious Mind

I know this may sound complicated. What the heck is subconscious reprogramming? Even better, what is a subconscious? That is definitely a question most will ask. I sure did.

Learning the definition of the subconscious and the difference between the subconscious and the conscious minds helped me to fully understand how important my thoughts were. It gave me a better understanding of the importance of the mind and what we allow into it. From as young as infants our subconscious is being shaped.

Our belief system begins to form and assign judgment to people, places and things. For example, if we are spanked as a young child for talking too much. We form the subconscious belief that talking too much is bad and we will be punished for it. Thus, we make a conscious effort throughout our lives to minimize our words.

Some of us were warned by our parents and grandparents to "beware" of sickness and disease, because many in our family had died before us of specific diseases that were believed to run in the family. Subconsciously we fear becoming sick and dying of these diseases. These fears are ingrained with-in us and most of us don't even realize we have them.

I had studied so many scientists and authors who specialize in the subconscious mind and the general consensus amongst them is that our inner world affects our outer world. So many of the descendants before us knew this fact. Why weren't we taught this from birth? If our subconscious is so critical to our emotional advancement, why isn't this information taught as early as preschool? As irritated as I was that I did not know this information early in life, I am equally as grateful that I acquired it before I died.

For years, I believed my mother who had abandoned me as a baby could heal me if she would just call and apologize for allowing drugs to consume her life. Her negative choices prevented her from being capable of being a good mother to me and my five siblings. I spent years feeling unworthy and unwanted because of her choice to abandon and abuse her children. The story I was told of her putting me into a suitcase as a three-month-old baby and closing it, leaving me for dead, haunted me for years. Knowing this fact caused me to grow up with severe self-worth issues and random bouts of depression. Her actions caused me to form the subconscious belief that I was not valuable and worthy of life. I formed the belief that if my own mother did not see value in me then no one would. This is the very belief that I would need to reprogram. Learning that this was necessary and taking the steps to reprogram that belief was half the battle won. Unfortunately, I did not begin that process until I was forty years old. I am open and transparent in my books so others can begin the healing process sooner than I did.

Throughout my life I never once remember someone approaching me and reminding me that I was unwanted by my own mother, not once. Most of the people in my life during my twenties and thirties had no idea about my past. The only time I heard that horrible story of abandonment was when I told it to myself. Inside I would say, "SaBrina, you don't deserve love because your mother didn't love you." I was the only one guilty of that. I also chose to take my mother's actions personally. She was an addict who doesn't even remember most of the horrible things she did. In no way am I excusing her behavior, but I am pointing out how we can carry hurt and pain for so many years from people who are not sharing that weight. We are the only ones suffering, and internal suffering is damaging to our mental and physical health. Suffering is a choice we do not have to make. After studying

Don Miguel Ruiz's concepts on not taking things personally in "The Four Agreements," I slowly began to change my perception of her actions. Her actions were more about her and her own mental darkness than they were about me. This helped me to slowly develop self worth. No one deserves to travel through life feeling like they do not matter, especially when those feelings are provoked by the actions of other human beings.

On June 18, 2018, my biological mother died. I did not know how to feel. For years, I would always say that I couldn't care less if she died, so I didn't expect to feel anything when I received the news of her death. On the contrary, I was suddenly struck with crippling pain. I felt it engulf me from the ground up and I could not stop it nor did I understand why it was there. I didn't love her. I didn't even know her. Because of her drug addiction I was never given the opportunity to love her. She definitely didn't love me. So why was I in pain?

Now in tears, I became angry that I was hurting. I thought to myself who hurts and sheds tears for a mother that never loved them? Who hurts for a mother that tried to kill them? What the heck is wrong with me? Why am I crying? I was mad and stuck in one place. I literally could not move. This unwanted emotion consumed me. I don't remember who I called first or how I finally moved from that position, but I did make a few phone calls. It felt unusual because all those in my life that were close to me knew that I did not have a relationship with my mother. I recall a friend telling me that what I was experiencing was called DNA pain. I didn't want it and I was resentful that it appeared even in death that my mother still had some emotional hold over me. I vowed at that moment that I would not be attending the funeral.

As the days went by, I learned about even more unacceptable abusive things my mother had done and had not made amends for. I was angry and I was happy she was dead. I began to feel grateful that I was not aware of all of the hurt and devastation she had caused our family. I was certain that God had intervened and protected me from all the facts because I most certainly would have felt compelled to confront her and force her to rectify her wrong doings. I began to feel that I had been spared from knowing exactly how evil she was. I understand to some that may sound harsh, but I have to be completely transparent in order for you to understand the dark state of mind I had to heal from.

Those feelings of gratitude were short-lived, and eventually I began to get depressed, which infuriated me. Thoughts of suicide and unworthiness returned. I had not been depressed in years. I had done so much emotional work over the years and I could not believe that this death was erasing all of that. I can only assume that there must have been a deep secret part of me that held out hope that she would finally lick all of our mental and emotional wounds and heal all of our hearts one day. I was wrong. After finding out that my mother had been in hospice care for months and was aware that she was dying, yet didn't reach out to her six children to apologize for her abandonment and abusive behavior. I was devastated all over again. I felt like all the work I had done to heal myself had been wasted.

I am not exactly sure what changed. I have no idea why I suddenly woke up one day and decided to speak at my mother's funeral. It must have been God, but I woke up one morning and decided I needed to participate in her funeral. I began communicating with my older sister and helped to arrange an obituary that was a little more honest than the one that had originally been created by my younger sister. The first line of her version of the obituary said "Shirley Ann Tillman was a great mother." What? "Are you kidding me," I thought. "Why would you write something that is a complete lie." I was not trying to be mean, but why would we ever say that she was a great mother in her obituary? She allowed me to create a more realistic version of the obituary. It wasn't my goal to bash my mother, I simply wanted to get this process over with so I could move on with my life, especially since I felt her death was putting me back at square one emotionally. I contacted some of her living relatives from Texas and asked them for true and honest characteristics of her personality. Some said she was a loyal friend, so I added that. The day of her funeral, the venue was filled with my Eastern Star sisters and Masonic brothers who all showed up for me because I needed support and pallbearers.

The service was eulogized by Bishop Reginald Black Sr., who is a great personal friend of mine as well as my Mason brother. My oldest sister,

Mary, and my two younger sisters, Verdell and Kaylen (Esther Jean), were in attendance. We were not able to locate the youngest of my mother's children. Kristen Latrell. To this day I don't know how long it was before she got the news of our mothers death. My mother was a member of the Junior Blind, and many of her friends from there were in attendance. I allowed everyone who wanted to give remarks to do so before me. I began my speech with, "These tears are not for Shirley Ann Tillman, these tears are for the six babies that suffered at her hands." I turned to my sisters who were seated to the left of me and said, "I'm sorry for the distance that has been created, and the wars that have been waged amongst us by our mother." I reminded them that the source of our pain is now gone, and we are now responsible for how we interact with and love each other from here on out. We can no longer blame our mother for the lives we choose to live. "She is gone," I said. "It is now up to us to build positive productive relationships with each other and live happy healthy lives and move forward."

I realize my speech in no way resembled the typical "Everyone is going to Heaven" funeral speech. I felt it was necessary for the closure I needed to continue on and finally put this all behind me. My mother's death left me with the realization that I still had a lot of healing to do.

At times, this mental and emotional transformation process is a long one. Reprogramming negative thought patterns, especially ones left by past trauma can take a long time. That is why it's best to begin working on them as soon as you identify each one. The time spent identifying and reversing negative thinking won't be in vain. It will truly change your life for the better.

One huge subconscious belief that I had to work overtime to reverse was the fact that specific major diseases seem to run in my family. This is a common subconscious acceptance for many. Because my biological mother had diabetes, every time I experienced any bodily discomfort, I was certain it was the onset of diabetes. I no longer believe in genetic predisposition to disease.

In the book "Feeling is the Secret," by Neville Goddard, he refers to the conscious as male and the subconscious as female. He points out that the woman, being the subconscious, has no desire to change the man, being the conscious. She simply accepts him as is. The subconscious mind does not judge what we plant with our conscious actions. If you spend all of your time telling yourself that you are poor and pitiful then that is the state of mind you will remain in. The universe will create even more situations for you to feel exactly that way. You can change your state of mind.

Feeling a certain way produces that state of mind. Feeling sad will produce sadness, feeling happy will produce happiness. The minute you identify bad feelings, do everything you can to change them. Take charge of your mood.

When I read books and I find the same concepts and beliefs that I believe in today, it's always a confirmation. It makes me feel great. It confirms that I'm on the right path. It solidifies in my mind that the knowledge is real and it's not new. Many great people had this knowledge years before any of us were ever born. This knowledge is not "new aged." It's clear that many of our ancestors possessed this great information. We must always be mindful of what we are planting in our subconscious mind because our subconscious mind will produce exactly what we believe we are. If at any point we want to change the information that we are giving to the subconscious, we have to consciously take steps to create a new picture and feel the emotions related to the new positive picture we have created. Act as if the things we desire are already happening now, not in the future, but now!

It can take years to master this concept, but doing so will change your life. Hoping and wishing does not produce a happy, prosperous life. Continuously hoping and begging God for the desires of our heart is a clear representation of lack and the fact that you have accepted that limitation. Instead, mentally pretend. Believe that it is already done. Allow your prayers to be prayers of gratitude. Act as if the things you desire have already shown up in your life and soon, they will.

The mind is a magical gift from God given to us to create our lives as we choose. Embrace your Mind and its magnificent power. Whatever has shown up thus far in your life is because you have consciously or subconsciously held those thoughts in your mind. Continue to do that intentionally and you will become the master of your fate.

@In59Seconds

The mind is like water.
When it is turbulent, it's difficult to see.
When it is calm, everything becomes clear.

-**Buddha**

Ten

We Must Recognize-Reject-Replace

It was a warm Sunday afternoon in 2012. I was enjoying the company of my oldest daughter Joi, who was seventeen years old at the time and a twelfth grade student at St. Mary's Academy (Blue Tie). She and I always have a great relationship. On this day she and I were walking around the track at Norman O. Houston park, not far from our home and I suddenly got a debilitating cramp in my lower abdomen. My daughter was instantly frightened and concerned. She asked, *"Mom are you okay?"* I couldn't answer because I was trying to breathe and allow the cramps to subside.

Once it passed, she and I gave each other an odd look and continued walking around the track. I hadn't been feeling my best, so I was attempting to return to a regular workout regimen because according to Google, the symptoms I had been experiencing were very similar to diabetes. I had been experiencing severe nausea, blurred vision, and frequent trips to the bathroom. My biological mother was an insulin-dependent diabetic, so I was afraid that genetics had caught up with me. I figured if that was the case, I should get a head start on the disease before I went to the doctor for an official diagnosis.

We continued walking when my daughter asked, *"Mom do you think there is any chance you may be pregnant?"* I looked at her and laughed hysterically. I said, *"Baby, I am forty-two years old. I have given birth to three children. Don't you think I would know my body well enough that if I were pregnant, I would definitely know? Furthermore, what do you know about pregnancy anyway?"* We laughed and continued exercising.

The thought of pregnancy wasn't even realistic in my mind. I had reached an age where things in women become inconsistent, I was past the age where one even considers pregnancy, and I was working out and getting my mind and body ready for my self-diagnosed diabetes, which I was certain I had inherited from my biological mother.

Eventually, my symptoms got so bad that I went to the emergency room at Gardena Memorial Hospital. Once I was brought into the nurse, she asked the standard question *"What brings you here today?"* I replied, *"I already know what's wrong, diabetes runs in my family and I'm just about positive I have it."* I pulled out a list that I had brought with me of all the facts and symptoms about diabetes that I had gotten off the internet. I showed the list to her and she gave me a strange look.

She then asked, *"Ms. Reece, is there any chance you could be pregnant?"* I said, *"No, no ma'am, I'm forty-two years old, those days are long gone for me."*

She said, *"Well, Ms. Ole' Lady, we still have to do a standard pregnancy test."*

I agreed, but I told her it was a complete waste of time because I was too old to be pregnant. My youngest child was 11 at the time and I hadn't had a normal menstrual cycle in years.

They proceeded with the test, but the emergency room was extremely crowded, so it took hours. I had also convinced them that I could possibly have gallstones because I did feel something weird in my stomach. Just as they were going to send me upstairs to have an ultrasound to look for gallstones or other causes for pain in my stomach, a nurse came in and said, *"Ms. Reece..."* By that time, I was lying down, attempting to sleep. I sat up and said, *"Yes?"* She said, *"Ms. Reece, you're pregnant!"*

Time stood still. My brain began to race, I replied, *"No, I'm not! That's precisely why I'm here, because I'm not pregnant, but I have all these symptoms."* She looked at me and realized I wasn't prepared to receive what she was saying, so she turned around and walked out of the room. About ten minutes later, she returned with the doctor and another nurse with the positive pregnancy test in hand. Once again, she said, "Ms. Reece, you are pregnant!"

I could not believe my ears. I began to sweat, and my mind began to race. I immediately started thinking about a glass of wine I had with dinner. Pregnant at forty-two. No way. I was in shock. The ultrasound that had been scheduled to search for gallstones was then changed, and I was sent upstairs to see the newfound fetus. Much to my surprise, I was not only definitely pregnant, I was 14 weeks pregnant. This was April 18, 2012.

I celebrated my 43rd Birthday on August 7, 2012 while on bed rest and exactly six months from the day I found out about her, on Oct, 18th 2012, a beautiful healthy baby girl whom I named Journey Schy Morris made her **unexpected journey** into the world and into our hearts.

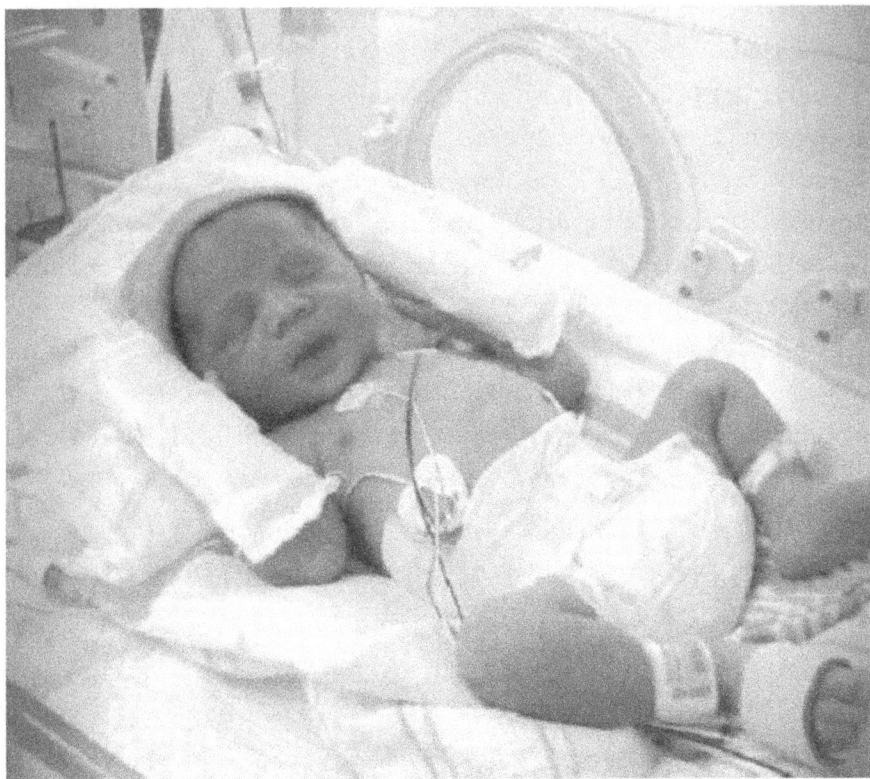

Journey Schy Morris, born October 18, 2012

I told this story because I want you to realize how strong subconscious beliefs can be. I sincerely believed that I had diabetes and that belief existed because of my knowledge of my biological mother having this illness. I believed that it was my genetic destiny to develop the same disease. When instead there

94

was a beautiful blessing growing inside of me.

Let's try hard not to block the Amazing blessings that God had for us because we are uncompromising in our beliefs. It's very possible this little life was moving inside of me, but I dismissed the fluttering feelings as something else because my belief in eventually becoming diabetic was stronger than my belief in the possibility of naturally becoming pregnant at age forty-two. Our subconscious beliefs can be strong and unshakable which is why we must attack them one by one and dissect them to make sure they are serving us well. Our beliefs need to be in line with exactly what we desire for our lives. You can't say you want to start a business but have a secret hidden belief that you will fail at that business. You can't say you desire a loving mate but deep inside of you there is a belief that you will never find a good mate. The deep-rooted subconscious belief will win every time.

God's plan for us may be perfect health but we "Believe" we are supposed to suffer from sickness and disease because our past relatives did. Therefore, because of the free will the Creator gave us to design our own lives, despite God's plan for great health for us, disease shows up instead. Many of us are taught by our parents and grandparents that we are doomed to develop the diseases of our ancestors and I clearly believed that for many years. I no longer share that belief. Despite the fact that certain genetic markers may be present, I no longer believe that we are genetically predisposed to disease. I know now that God gave all human beings the ability to transcend those apparent genetic sick genes with our minds. ***Your mind is magic!***

The mind is amazingly powerful. It is so powerful, that although I had symptoms of pregnancy, I ignored them because of my subconscious programming. Baby Journey was growing inside of me, yet my mind had convinced me of something completely different. Even when I felt typical pregnancy symptoms like fatigue, frequent urination, and nausea, I ignored them and diagnosed myself with something else that was easier to believe in. Remember the bible says, *"It is done unto you as you believe."* So, recognizing what our true beliefs are is vital. The things that show up in your life are based solely off of your belief system. Take some time to figure out exactly what you believe.

Mind is all. We must identify what we truly believe. I no longer believe in the possibilities of long term sickness and disease. I reinforce that with daily affirmations by saying,

"Sickness and disease do not live in my body."
"I am healthy and wealthy in all areas of my life."

Perfect health is a concept that I want everyone in the world to adopt. Mentally embrace the concept of perfect health. Even when physical ailments are present. View them as temporary, just passing through your body, possibly to slow us down and bring awareness to something God wants us to pay attention to, but do not mentally accept them as permanent.

Studying the placebo effect helped me to confirm my belief that sickness is optional. I am definitely not asking anyone to stop taking your prescribed medication or ignore advice given by your doctor. I am merely suggesting that you take your medicine and follow the physician's orders with an optimistic mindset. Believing that you are already healed.

Make no mistake, although I sincerely do not believe that sickness and disease have to be a deathly fate for anyone or even a physically debilitating one. There still seems to be times when unfortunate physical situations happen no matter how evolved we believe ourselves to be. Several times throughout my forties, I experienced high blood pressure and had to be put on medication. I was so against it that I removed myself from it for two years and replaced the medicine with exercise, ginger root and apple cider vinegar. I would never be irresponsible or suggest to anyone to stop taking their medication. I do believe it was my strong belief in the alternative measures that I was taking that allowed me to be successful in staying off medicine for two years and not having any complications. I honestly understand why medical doctors warn about genetic predisposition to illness, however it is my strong opinion that despite genetic markers and despite statistics, the Mind has the ability to transcend all sickness and disease. Take your medication but take it with the belief that whatever physical ailment you are experiencing is temporary and simply passes through your body on its way out.

How grateful I was that I had spent years strengthening that belief in perfect health. In late 2019, after waking up from a surgery to remove my tonsils, adenoids and re-open my eardrum, I was told that when going into my ear to drain what they believed to be a cyst with the hopes of re-opening my eardrum and restoring the 30% hearing loss that I was experiencing in my left ear, that what they thought was a harmless cyst was actually a tumor and would require brain surgery to remove.

Initially, despite my daily attempts to remain positive, I was disappointed that someone who completely rejects the idea of sickness could receive a diagnosis like this.

Acoustic Neuroma; a benign tumor that sits on the hearing and facial nerves in the brain. I was told my tumor had also wrapped itself around my facial nerves, so removing it could cause partial facial paralysis. The idea of that was very unsettling. I was afraid.

Sometimes you want to scream and ask God, "Why isn't my life perfect?"

Why weren't my affirmations working? I was no different than other people who became doubtful and afraid, but the only significant difference was that I knew the danger of staying in that place. I remember being sad and having a "Why me?" pity party. I even made a video about it, but soon after, I quickly started allowing the gratitude to change my attitude. I was grateful that the tumor was not only found, but most importantly, not cancerous. Once I began to focus on the positive in the situation, I felt much better. Shortly after my initial surgery and diagnosis, I traveled to Istanbul, Turkey, and Athens, Delphi, Meteora and Santorini, Greece, and I had a magnificent time.

I had a few friends that begged me not to go due to their fear of the pressure of flying affecting the tumor, but I was not going to live or think in fear. Not only did I go on the wonderful trip, I didn't experience the pain during the flight that my doctor told me to expect. I enjoyed all of these beautiful cities with women that I have grown to love dearly. Many of whom I have also traveled with to Indonesia, Peru, and Egypt. These women have become my family. We all still keep in touch and continue to cultivate our positive relationships currently. I love them all dearly.

Athens Greece. November, 2019

When I returned home from my trip, I made an appointment with the neurosurgeon and moved forward with a hopeful, more positive attitude.

I began to focus on my belief in sound healing and spend a lot of time meditating to specific sounds such as 432 and 528 megahertz binary tones. I bought a key of #A pineal sound bowl, which I absolutely love, and a tuning fork. I set an intention to visualize the tumor shrinking each time I used the sound bowl and fork.

Belief is Everything when you make a choice to create and implement positive practices in your life it is vital that you believe wholeheartedly in them. On my second visit to the neurosurgeon after careful study of my MRI images. Dr. Sean Xin confirmed that no brain surgery is needed. He said the location of the tumor is slightly outside of the brain, which will require only a simple, noninvasive, less critical surgery that can be done by an ear, nose, and throat specialist.

Although the concept of self-healing is new to me, I believe in it strongly. I believe God gave us everything we need on this earth to nourish and heal our own bodies. The ancestors before us knew the healing properties of this amazing planet. I'm excited about learning more about natural herbs and how they benefit the human body, but what I'm certain of is the trust in nature's remedies must still be coupled with the strong mental belief in them.

Do I believe that my thought process coupled with my daily positive habitual practices are responsible for the outcome of my medical situation? Absolutely! God gave us the amazing power to create an image in our minds of perfection. We have been equipped with all the tools we need to design a magnificent life, free of illness. I will spend the rest of my life mastering these tools and teaching others to do the same.

There have been a few other times in my life where I felt God's amazing divine energy intervened on my behalf. When I began branding myself as a motivational speaker, I would make sure to attend every seminar that came to town. Les Brown, whom I have studied extensively from the time I decided I wanted to speak, was in Los Angeles for an empowerment seminar called, "Get Motivated." I couldn't wait to attend the event. A couple of my Toastmasters friends were going as well. We weren't able to get seats in the front, which would have been my preference, but we all happily settled in on row 17. There were many speakers that came on before Les Brown, but I was patiently awaiting his arrival. He was my inspiration. I am certain I had seen every single motivational video he had made, and I was honored to see him speak in person.

Hours went by and suddenly I saw an old friend of mine walking down the center aisle. I got up to speak to her and she was just as thrilled to see me as I was her. We hugged and I briefly told her that I was a motivational speaker now. She asked where I was sitting. I pointed to the seventeenth row. She said, "Girl, I'm bringing you to the front with me." I told her I had a couple of friends with me. She eventually moved all my friends to the second and third rows as well. When it was time for Les Brown to come out, she literally had someone take a chair and place it in the front row directly in front of Les Brown center stage. I could not believe it. There I was, seated directly in front of the man whose words aided in my mental and spiritual transformation over the past few years. It was as if God said, "You are great, let Me place you in the seat of greatness." I recognized the blessing instantly. I was so grateful for my friends' efforts. I later asked her, "Did you know I was an aspiring motivational speaker before today?" She said she had no clue. She had never seen my motivational Youtube videos. God uses people, places, and things to make our dreams come true. Divine intervention at its finest took place that day. I was completely OK with being in the back. I was just happy to be there, but God said, "Nope, this is my gift to you," which made me feel like I was definitely on the correct path for my life. I sat filled with gratitude and thrilled by the confirmation that God will grant you the desires of your heart. That day, July 29, 2015, I was a true recipient of God's favor, without a doubt. I have never doubted that I would be a famous, life changing motivational and inspirational speaker one day, but it sure feels good when the universe conspires to grant you your heart's desires.

I recognized this immediately as manifestation. On this day, in that room was exactly where I was supposed to be. I knew I had called this moment into existence with my thoughts. On so many occasions I had thought of meeting Les Brown and now here I was in a seat made just for me staring up at the famous Les Brown.

Me, SaBrina Fisher Reece sitting in front of Les Brown

The Number 33

My oldest daughter has always believed in numerology. I wasn't a non-believer, but I simply had not given it much thought. I live in South Los Angeles, where the popular rapper, Nipsey Hussle owned a store called "The

Marathon." His store was located within walking distance from my home. There was a burger place located in the same shopping center of his store, but I rarely went there because there were always a lot of guys hanging out. Unfortunately, in 2019, Nipsey was shot and killed directly in front of his place of business. This outraged the community and there was an abundance of neighborhood support.

While the world was watching his widely televised funeral I chose not to initially. I always wake up in the early morning somewhere between 3:00 and 4:00 am. One morning shortly after 3:00 AM, as usual I woke up and for some strange reason, I logged onto my Youtube and began finally watching what the majority of the world had already seen a few days prior. While watching the funeral video, I discovered that Nipsey had died at age *thirty-three*. Since his death I noticed him frequently being compared to Jesus Christ, who had also been killed at age *thirty-three*. I remember thinking how unusual that was. I continued watching the funeral footage. While doing so I began to receive notifications to my personal youtube channel. I clicked the notifications and many of them were comments from people who had viewed a video of mine that had been posted approximately two years prior. The title of the video is "Motivational Speaker SaBrina Fisher Reece speaking at KRST Unity Center of Afrakan Spiritual Science." I clicked onto my video and my eyes were immediately drawn to the "likes." It had been liked *thirty-three* times. The notifications were comments all saying things like, "Nipsey Hussle's mother sent me here." Nipsey's mother was a member of KRST, and had mentioned the Unity Center during the funeral.

I went to wake up my daughter because I knew she would find these numerical similarities interesting, and as I handed her my phone, I noticed that my battery life read *33%*. I looked at her in disbelief. I said "There is no way this is all coincidence. She found it intriguing and when she woke up that morning, she researched the number **33** and texted it to me. When I received her text it was 7:**33**am.

I became an instant believer in numerology. After studying and researching the number **33** we found that it is known to be a Master Number, and resonates with the energies of compassion, blessings, inspiration, honesty, discipline, bravery and courage. According to several experts in this field, the number **33** tells us that 'all things are possible.' It is said that the number **33** is also the number that symbolizes guidance. I am not exactly sure what I believe the connection to be, but I am certain that on that particular day I was meant to acknowledge the connection. I have my own interpretation of why it happened. It could be as simple as the universe letting me know that I am on the correct spiritual path. Perception is relative, but I choose to believe that God was attempting to deliver a message. I believe the message was simply confirming that I am on the right spiritual path.

At the very least, it opened my mind to the possibility that everything is connected. I can only assume that as I continue to grow spiritually the numerical, spiritual, geometric, astrological and other connections will all become clear to me. I'm looking forward to connecting all the dots.

Eleven

You Will Feel It

We have all heard the phrase, "Fake it until you make it," but I have further expanded on the meaning of that since I have learned the importance of feeling. Now, I choose to say, "Fake it until you *feel* it." Once we begin utilizing personal development tools like imagination, creative visualization and affirmations, we realize that sometimes when we buckle down to begin the process we aren't always in the best mood. We may be preparing to say the affirmation: "I am happy and healthy, I am happy and healthy," but at that very moment we don't feel happy or healthy. My suggestion is to go stand in front of a mirror and repeat it anyway. Fake the feeling, pretend as children do. As you continue to speak this powerful affirmation to yourself in the mirror repeatedly, you will eventually begin to actually feel that way. The consistent affirmative stance will transform the negative feeling into a positive one. Positivity wins every time.

I realize many of us are quite busy with our lives and do not feel we have time for long drawn out positive affirmation sessions. That is why I created the #In59seconds Movement. A simple 59 seconds each day of positivity can and will change our lives. While you're running around getting dressed to begin your day. Take 59 seconds to speak to the universe. Speak the perfect day you desire into existence. Tell yourself, "I feel great today, Today is beautiful. Today is a happy day. Today I will make a lot of money. Today everyone will be happy to see me." It does not have to consume a lot of your time. Just 59 seconds of uplifting fuel will do the trick. It can be the very boost you need to ensure a productive day. Use that same 59 seconds to encourage others. Tell your children they are amazing and they have the ability to accomplish anything. Tell your spouse how much you appreciate them and how attractive they look today. This small amount of time of positive empowerment can make a difference in your life and the lives of others. The #In59Seconds Movement can motivate the world.

Words are energy and it has been my experience that repeatedly saying an affirmation aloud will eventually invoke the feeling, and the feeling is the last puzzle piece. Just try it, you have absolutely nothing to lose. Once we couple the positive words with the feelings, that is when the magic of manifestation happens. We must combine the consistent speaking of the words with the feeling of actually having what we desire. This is the perfect recipe to create a great life for yourself.

Many unfortunate situations can and will happen in life. When we allow ourselves to feel bad, we lower our energetic vibration. Despite how justified we are in negatively reacting to a bad situation. We still cannot allow ourselves to stay in the negative state of mind. Thinking negatively lowers our energetic vibration. If we are vibrating at a low frequency then we will attract all things that are also vibrating at that low level. That is why it is vital to learn to raise our vibration as soon as we wake up in the morning. We can raise our own vibration and it's imperative that we do so before we leave the house.

Gospel music is a tool I use daily to feel better. Quite often when I wake up in the morning, my mind is instantly flooded with what bills are due, who I'm upset with, who has disappointed me, what responsibilities I have for the day. Yes, It can be overwhelming. But it's crucial that we do not allow those feelings to continue. We can choose to change how we perceive things. Yes, bills and other financial responsibilities exist however we do not have to perceive them as problems. I now train myself to start thanking God that I have a home to pay a mortgage on rather than being annoyed that the mortgage is due. Instead of agonizing over paying my monthly car note, I remind myself that many don't have vehicles and I continuously put my mind in a state of gratitude that It has always been blessed to have a nice one.

We were born with the natural ability to feel good. We produce natural serotonin in our brains. Serotonin is a chemical messenger that is believed to act as a mood stabilizer. It helps us sleep better. Studies show that high serotonin levels are linked to feeling good and living longer, which should be an ultimate goal for us all.

There are certain foods that increase our body's production of serotonin. Specialists in this field encourage people to eat these specific foods that have been proven to raise the level of serotonin in our bodies. According to the expert these foods include eggs, cheese, pineapples, tofu, salmon, nuts and seeds, and turkey. It may be beneficial to study these foods and others that stimulate serotonin production and choose which of these foods fit best into your daily lifestyle.

When our serotonin levels are low, we may feel irritable, anxious, depressed, pessimistic and experience irregular sleeping patterns. On the contrary, when our serotonin levels are high, we feel happy, energized, and hopeful. Doesn't everyone want to feel happy?

Natural ways to increase serotonin include exercise, cold showers, natural sunshine, prayer, meditation, singing, dancing, and speaking positive affirmations. There isn't just one way. Find what tools work for you and what compliments your lifestyle and practice it daily. Do not view this practice as a chore. Allow yourself to view participating in these daily practices as you willfully doing something daily to enhance the quality of your life. Even when you simply don't feel it, fake it! Do it anyway. You would be surprised how quickly your feelings will turn around.

I love working out, but sometimes I am lazy, and I simply do not want to do it. I find that if I force myself to get up anyway, shortly after beginning I start to feel so good about myself. Instantly I'll start to see that I have elevated my mood or raised my vibration by pushing myself to do it anyway. Raising one's vibration simply means choosing to operate at a higher frequency. Being happy versus sad, energetic versus a lack of energy, being hopeful versus choosing to focus on all your problems.

The concept of *"fake it until you feel it"* in no way means be unauthentic. It plainly means act as if you feel good until you do. Act as if you want to work out and eventually you will be so grateful that you did. Act as if you have abundance in your life and one day you will. Choose to act pleasant in public as opposed to acting grumpy. Get up and go out into the world and act happy and shortly you will forget that you weren't. Most importantly, you will attract others who are attempting to be positive as well.

When we are parents it is vital that we don't bombard our children with negative phrases like, "This is a horrible day," or "Life sucks." They are listening to our every word. Whether we like or not, they are mentally recording the things they hear us say. To me, this is more of a reason to "fake it". Your five-year-old need not hear the doom and gloom of your life. We owe them a fair chance at happiness, and if all they hear from us is a negative picture of the world, they will begin to feel that way themselves, which is grossly unfair to a child. Show them love and smiles, days filled with happiness and joy and they will grow into happy adults.

There is always something to be grateful for, and expressing that gratitude usually makes you feel better. Let gratitude change your attitude, and in doing so you will learn to drop all those negative labels you put on yourself, and soon you will find yourself becoming a cheerful, motivated, and happy person whom others want to be around.

When I first began speaking motivationally, I had absolutely no experience whatsoever. Other than the few speeches I had given in my Toastmasters International Club, I was a complete novice. Despite being a complete beginner, I started branding myself as a successful motivational speaker. I began dressing the part. I had a professional photo shoot done. I dressed like a speaker. When I walked into a room that I was to deliver a speech in, I was always super nervous. My heart felt like it was going to jump out of my chest each time, yet I walked in the room with confidence. I faked it until I felt it. People would compliment me and give me feedback and called me a seasoned speaker, but I was far from it. Eventually I became that talented, well-seasoned speaker that I pretended to be. I faked it until I was it. In my mind's eye, I saw myself on stage speaking to huge crowds.

I studied other great speakers. I hired several speaking coaches. I attended every speaking seminar I could find. Each year I would travel to attend the Toastmaster International World Championship of Public Speaking. I wanted to surround myself with other people who were doing exactly what I chose to do with the rest of my life. I ordered professional business cards with the words, "Motivational Speaker" in large letters across top of each card. I passed them out to everyone I came in contact with. I didn't introduce myself as SaBrina Fisher Reece, an "aspiring motivational speaker." I proudly greeted them saying "My name is SaBrina Fisher Reece, I am a motivational speaker." Believe in the unseen, act as if you already are exactly who you want to be. Fake it until you feel it and it will become a reality.

Throughout my journey of transformation if ever there was a time that I became discouraged and I was entertaining negative thoughts, I would pick up a book or watch a video by one of our legendary thought leaders. I have read so many books that date as far back as the very early 1900's. Some of my favorite influencers that seem to think very similar to me are: William Walker Atkinson, Eckhart Tolle, Don Miguel Ruiz, Norman Vincent Peale, Greg Braden, Earnest Holmes, Earl Nightingale, Zig Ziglar, W. Clement Stone, Marianne Williamson, Edgar Casey, Joseph Murphy, Nevelle Goodard, Ralph Waldo Emerson, Frederick J. Eikerenkoetter II (Rev. Ike), Joseph Murphy, Robert Collier, and many more. I trained myself to engulf myself in positive thinking whenever I would find myself returning to an old way of thinking. Doing this truly helps it to become a habitual practice. It can take years to retrain our brains and undo all of the negative programming we have lived with most of our lives, but it's vital that we all do it if we sincerely want to have a happy productive life.

The Will

There is something in each of us called, "The Will." The Will is that powerful driving force within us all that gives us the strength and determination to go after what we want. At times it may appear that others have a stronger will than we do. However, we can crank that inner knob on our own "Will" and turn it up to full speed at any point. William Walker Atkinson says, "The Will is the outward manifestation of the 'I Am.'" I completely agree. "I Am" is the most powerful phrase we can say. It leaves no room for future hope and wishes. The statement "I Am," represents now! It represents being completely in the current moment, not believing in or waiting for something to happen later but accepting it as already existing now. Understand the difference between being hopeful for something we desire in the future and claiming that thing to already exist in the present. Even if you can't see or touch it yet, fake it! Feel it! Express gratitude for it now. Act as if it is already there. If you are sad, act happy. If you are poor, act rich. Fake it until you actually feel it and it will soon materialize.

Many people have survived devastating circumstances because they had the will to live. We don't have to wait for a life or death situation to invoke our will. We are the fuel that powers up the Will. When we decide to go full force after our dreams, we find that we are stronger, smarter, and more driven than we could have ever imagined.

Twelve

Unexpected Journey

❧

It was a warm Sunday afternoon in 2012. I was enjoying the company of my oldest daughter Joi, who was seventeen years old at the time and a twelfth grade student at St. Mary's Academy (Blue Tie). She and I always have a great relationship. On this day she and I were walking around the track at Norman O. Houston park, not far from our home and I suddenly got a debilitating cramp in my lower abdomen. My daughter was instantly frightened and concerned. She asked, *"Mom are you okay?"* I couldn't answer because I was trying to breathe and allow the cramps to subside.

Once it passed, she and I gave each other an odd look and continued walking around the track. I hadn't been feeling my best, so I was attempting to return to a regular workout regimen because according to Google, the symptoms I had been experiencing were very similar to diabetes. I had been experiencing severe nausea, blurred vision, and frequent trips to the bathroom. My biological mother was an insulin-dependent diabetic, so I was afraid that genetics had caught up with me. I figured if that was the case, I should get a head start on the disease before I went to the doctor for an official diagnosis.

We continued walking when my daughter asked, *"Mom do you think there is any chance you may be pregnant?"* I looked at her and laughed hysterically. I said, *"Baby, I am forty-two years old. I have given birth to three children. Don't you think I would know my body well enough that if I were pregnant, I would definitely know? Furthermore, what do you know about pregnancy anyway?"* We laughed and continued exercising.

The thought of pregnancy wasn't even realistic in my mind. I had reached an age where things in women become inconsistent, I was past the age where one even considers pregnancy, and I was working out and getting my mind and body ready for my self-diagnosed diabetes, which I was certain I had inherited from my biological mother.

Eventually, my symptoms got so bad that I went to the emergency room at Gardena Memorial Hospital. Once I was brought into the nurse, she asked the standard question *"What brings you here today?"* I replied, *"I already know what's wrong, diabetes runs in my family and I'm just about positive I have it."* I pulled out a list that I had brought with me of all the facts and symptoms about diabetes that I had gotten off the internet. I showed the list to her and she gave me a strange look.

She then asked, *"Ms. Reece, is there any chance you could be pregnant?"* I said, *"No, no ma'am, I'm forty-two years old, those days are long gone for me."*

She said, *"Well, Ms. Ole' Lady, we still have to do a standard pregnancy test."*

I agreed, but I told her it was a complete waste of time because I was too old to be pregnant. My youngest child was 11 at the time and I hadn't had a normal menstrual cycle in years.

They proceeded with the test, but the emergency room was extremely crowded, so it took hours. I had also convinced them that I could possibly have gallstones because I did feel something weird in my stomach. Just as they were going to send me upstairs to have an ultrasound to look for gallstones or other causes for pain in my stomach, a nurse came in and said, *"Ms. Reece..."* By that time, I was lying down, attempting to sleep. I sat up and said, *"Yes?"* She said, *"Ms. Reece, you're pregnant!"*

Time stood still. My brain began to race, I replied, *"No, I'm not! That's precisely why I'm here, because I'm not pregnant, but I have all these symptoms."* She looked at me and realized I wasn't prepared to receive what she was saying, so she turned around and walked out of the room. About ten minutes later, she returned with the doctor and another nurse with the positive pregnancy test in hand. Once again, she said, "Ms. Reece, you are pregnant!"

I could not believe my ears. I began to sweat, and my mind began to race. I immediately started thinking about a glass of wine I had with dinner. Pregnant at forty-two. No way. I was in shock. The ultrasound that had been scheduled to search for gallstones was then changed, and I was sent upstairs to see the newfound fetus. Much to my surprise, I was not only definitely pregnant, I was 14 weeks pregnant. This was April 18, 2012.

I celebrated my 43rd Birthday on August 7, 2012 while on bed rest and exactly six months from the day I found out about her, on Oct, 18th 2012, a beautiful healthy baby girl whom I named Journey Schy Morris made her **unexpected journey** into the world and into our hearts.

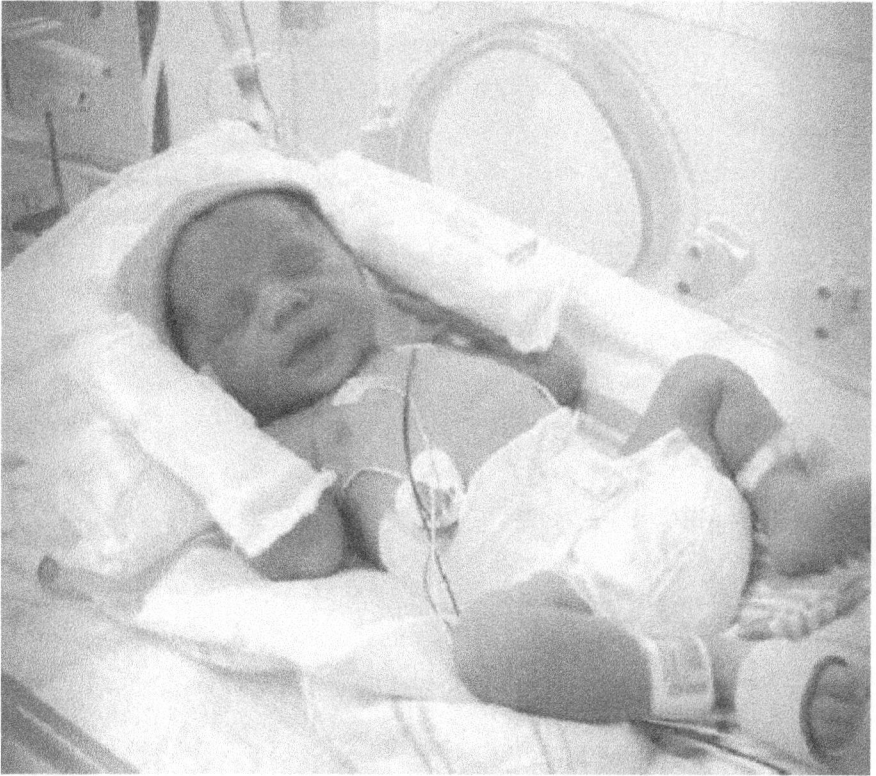

Journey Schy Morris, born October 18, 2012

I told this story because I want you to realize how strong subconscious beliefs can be. I sincerely believed that I had diabetes and that belief existed because of my knowledge of my biological mother having this illness. I believed that it was my genetic destiny to develop the same disease. When instead there was a beautiful blessing growing inside of me.

Let's try hard not to block the Amazing blessings that God had for us because we are uncompromising in our beliefs. It's very possible this little life was moving inside of me, but I dismissed the fluttering feelings as something else because my belief in eventually becoming diabetic was stronger than my belief in the possibility of naturally becoming pregnant at age forty-two. Our subconscious beliefs can be strong and unshakable which is why we must attack them one by one and dissect them to make sure they are serving us well. Our beliefs need to be in line with exactly what we desire for our lives. You can't say you want to start a business but have a secret hidden belief that you will fail at that business. You can't say you desire a loving mate but deep inside of you there is a belief that you will never find a good mate. The deep-rooted subconscious belief will win every time.

God's plan for us may be perfect health but we "Believe" we are supposed to suffer from sickness and disease because our past relatives did. Therefore, because of the free will the Creator gave us to design our own lives, despite God's plan for great health for us, disease shows up instead. Many of us are taught by our parents and grandparents that we are doomed to develop the diseases of our ancestors and I clearly believed that for many years. I no longer share that belief. Despite the fact that certain genetic markers may be present, I no longer believe that we are genetically predisposed to disease. I know now that God gave all human beings the ability to transcend those apparent genetic sick genes with our minds. ***Your mind is magic!***

The mind is amazingly powerful. It is so powerful, that although I had symptoms of pregnancy, I ignored them because of my subconscious programming. Baby Journey was growing inside of me, yet my mind had convinced me of something completely different. Even when I felt typical pregnancy symptoms like fatigue, frequent urination, and nausea, I ignored them and diagnosed myself with something else that was easier to believe in. Remember the bible says, *"It is done unto you as you believe."* So, recognizing what our true beliefs are is vital. The things that show up in your life are based solely off of your belief system. Take some time to figure out exactly what you believe.

Mind is all. We must identify what we truly believe. I no longer believe in the possibilities of long term sickness and disease. I reinforce that with daily affirmations by saying,

> *"Sickness and disease do not live in my body."*
> *"I am healthy and wealthy in all areas of my life."*

Perfect health is a concept that I want everyone in the world to adopt. Mentally embrace the concept of perfect health. Even when physical ailments are present. View them as temporary, just passing through your body, possibly to slow us down and bring awareness to something God wants us to pay attention to, but do not mentally accept them as permanent.

Studying the placebo effect helped me to confirm my belief that sickness is optional. I am definitely not asking anyone to stop taking your prescribed medication or ignore advice given by your doctor. I am merely suggesting that you take your medicine and follow the physician's orders with an optimistic mindset. Believing that you are already healed.

Make no mistake, although I sincerely do not believe that sickness and disease have to be a deathly fate for anyone or even a physically debilitating one. There still seems to be times when unfortunate physical situations happen no matter how evolved we believe ourselves to be. Several times throughout my forties, I experienced high blood pressure and had to be put on medication. I was so against it that I removed myself from it for two years and replaced the medicine with exercise, ginger root and apple cider vinegar. I would never be irresponsible or suggest to anyone to stop taking their medication. I do believe it was my strong belief in the alternative measures that I was taking that allowed me to be successful in staying off medicine for two years and not having any complications. I honestly understand why medical doctors warn about genetic predisposition to illness, however it is my strong opinion that despite genetic markers and despite statistics, the Mind has the ability to transcend all sickness and disease. Take your medication but take it with the belief that whatever physical ailment you are experiencing is temporary and simply passes through your body on its way out.

How grateful I was that I had spent years strengthening that belief in perfect health. In late 2019, after waking up from a surgery to remove my tonsils, adenoids and re-open my eardrum, I was told that when going into my ear to drain what they believed to be a cyst with the hopes of re-opening my eardrum and restoring the 30% hearing loss that I was experiencing in my left ear, that what they thought was a harmless cyst was actually a tumor and would require brain surgery to remove.

Initially, despite my daily attempts to remain positive, I was disappointed that someone who completely rejects the idea of sickness could receive a diagnosis like this.

Acoustic Neuroma; a benign tumor that sits on the hearing and facial nerves in the brain. I was told my tumor had also wrapped itself around my facial nerves, so removing it could cause partial facial paralysis. The idea of that was very unsettling. I was afraid.

Sometimes you want to scream and ask God, "Why isn't my life perfect?"

Why weren't my affirmations working? I was no different than other people who became doubtful and afraid, but the only significant difference was that I knew the danger of staying in that place. I remember being sad and having a "Why me?" pity party. I even made a video about it, but soon after, I quickly started allowing the gratitude to change my attitude. I was grateful that the tumor was not only found, but most importantly, not cancerous. Once I began to focus on the positive in the situation, I felt much better. Shortly after my initial surgery and diagnosis, I traveled to Istanbul, Turkey, and Athens, Delphi, Meteora and Santorini, Greece, and I had a magnificent time.

I had a few friends that begged me not to go due to their fear of the pressure of flying affecting the tumor, but I was not going to live or think in fear. Not only did I go on the wonderful trip, I didn't experience the pain during the flight that my doctor told me to expect. I enjoyed all of these beautiful cities with women that I have grown to love dearly. Many of whom I have also traveled with to Indonesia, Peru, and Egypt. These women have become my family. We all still keep in touch and continue to cultivate our positive relationships currently. I love them all dearly.

Athens Greece. November, 2019

When I returned home from my trip, I made an appointment with the neurosurgeon and moved forward with a hopeful, more positive attitude.

I began to focus on my belief in sound healing and spend a lot of time meditating to specific sounds such as 432 and 528 megahertz binary tones. I bought a key of #A pineal sound bowl, which I absolutely love, and a tuning fork. I set an intention to visualize the tumor shrinking each time I used the sound bowl and fork.

Belief is Everything when you make a choice to create and implement positive practices in your life it is vital that you believe wholeheartedly in them. On my second visit to the neurosurgeon after careful study of my MRI images. Dr. Sean Xin confirmed that no brain surgery is needed. He said the location of the tumor is slightly outside of the brain, which will require only a simple, noninvasive, less critical surgery that can be done by an ear, nose, and throat specialist.

Although the concept of self-healing is new to me, I believe in it strongly. I believe God gave us everything we need on this earth to nourish and heal our own bodies. The ancestors before us knew the healing properties of this amazing planet. I'm excited about learning more about natural herbs and how they benefit the human body, but what I'm certain of is the trust in nature's remedies must still be coupled with the strong mental belief in them.

Do I believe that my thought process coupled with my daily positive habitual practices are responsible for the outcome of my medical situation? Absolutely! God gave us the amazing power to create an image in our minds of perfection. We have been equipped with all the tools we need to design a magnificent life, free of illness. I will spend the rest of my life mastering these tools and teaching others to do the same.

There have been a few other times in my life where I felt God's amazing divine energy intervened on my behalf. When I began branding myself as a motivational speaker, I would make sure to attend every seminar that came to town. Les Brown, whom I have studied extensively from the time I decided I wanted to speak, was in Los Angeles for an empowerment seminar called, "Get Motivated." I couldn't wait to attend the event. A couple of my Toastmasters friends were going as well. We weren't able to get seats in the front, which would have been my preference, but we all happily settled in on row 17. There were many speakers that came on before Les Brown, but I was patiently awaiting his arrival. He was my inspiration. I am certain I had seen every single motivational video he had made, and I was honored to see him speak in person.

Hours went by and suddenly I saw an old friend of mine walking down the center aisle. I got up to speak to her and she was just as thrilled to see me as I was her. We hugged and I briefly told her that I was a motivational speaker now. She asked where I was sitting. I pointed to the seventeenth row. She said, "Girl, I'm bringing you to the front with me." I told her I had a couple of friends with me. She eventually moved all my friends to the second and third rows as well. When it was time for Les Brown to come out, she literally had someone take a chair and place it in the front row directly in front of Les Brown center stage. I could not believe it. There I was, seated directly in front of the man whose words aided in my mental and spiritual transformation over the past few years. It was as if God said, "You are great, let Me place you in the seat of greatness." I recognized the blessing instantly. I was so grateful for my friends' efforts. I later asked her, "Did you know I was an aspiring motivational speaker before today?" She said she had no clue. She had never seen my motivational Youtube videos. God uses people, places, and things to make our dreams come true. Divine intervention at its finest took place that day. I was completely OK with being in the back. I was just happy to be there, but God said, "Nope, this is my gift to you," which made me feel like I was definitely on the correct path for my life. I sat filled with gratitude and thrilled by the confirmation that God will grant you the desires of your heart. That day, July 29, 2015, I was a true recipient of God's favor, without a doubt. I have never doubted that I would be a famous, life changing motivational and inspirational speaker one day, but it sure feels good when the universe conspires to grant you your heart's desires.

I recognized this immediately as manifestation. On this day, in that room was exactly where I was supposed to be. I knew I had called this moment into existence with my thoughts. On so many occasions I had thought of meeting Les Brown and now here I was in a seat made just for me staring up at the famous Les Brown.

Me, SaBrina Fisher Reece sitting in front of Les Brown

The Number 33

My oldest daughter has always believed in numerology. I wasn't a non-believer, but I simply had not given it much thought. I live in South Los Angeles, where the popular rapper, Nipsey Hussle owned a store called "The

Marathon." His store was located within walking distance from my home. There was a burger place located in the same shopping center of his store, but I rarely went there because there were always a lot of guys hanging out. Unfortunately, in 2019, Nipsey was shot and killed directly in front of his place of business. This outraged the community and there was an abundance of neighborhood support.

While the world was watching his widely televised funeral I chose not to initially. I always wake up in the early morning somewhere between 3:00 and 4:00 am. One morning shortly after 3:00 AM, as usual I woke up and for some strange reason, I logged onto my Youtube and began finally watching what the majority of the world had already seen a few days prior. While watching the funeral video, I discovered that Nipsey had died at age **thirty-three**. Since his death I noticed him frequently being compared to Jesus Christ, who had also been killed at age **thirty-three.** I remember thinking how unusual that was. I continued watching the funeral footage. While doing so I began to receive notifications to my personal youtube channel. I clicked the notifications and many of them were comments from people who had viewed a video of mine that had been posted approximately two years prior. The title of the video is "Motivational Speaker SaBrina Fisher Reece speaking at KRST Unity Center of Afrakan Spiritual Science." I clicked onto my video and my eyes were immediately drawn to the "likes." It had been liked **thirty-three** times. The notifications were comments all saying things like, "Nipsey Hussle's mother sent me here." Nipsey's mother was a member of KRST, and had mentioned the Unity Center during the funeral.

I went to wake up my daughter because I knew she would find these numerical similarities interesting, and as I handed her my phone, I noticed that my battery life read *33%*. I looked at her in disbelief. I said "There is no way this is all coincidence. She found it intriguing and when she woke up that morning, she researched the number **33** and texted it to me. When I received her text it was 7:**33**am.

I became an instant believer in numerology. After studying and researching the number **33** we found that it is known to be a Master Number, and resonates with the energies of compassion, blessings, inspiration, honesty, discipline, bravery and courage. According to several experts in this field, the number **33** tells us that 'all things are possible.' It is said that the number **33** is also the number that symbolizes guidance. I am not exactly sure what I believe the connection to be, but I am certain that on that particular day I was meant to acknowledge the connection. I have my own interpretation of why it happened. It could be as simple as the universe letting me know that I am on the correct spiritual path. Perception is relative, but I choose to believe that God was attempting to deliver a message. I believe the message was simply confirming that I am on the right spiritual path.

At the very least, it opened my mind to the possibility that everything is connected. I can only assume that as I continue to grow spiritually the numerical, spiritual, geometric, astrological and other connections will all become clear to me. I'm looking forward to connecting all the dots.

Thirteen

The Responsibility of Conscious Creation

"Man is all imagination, and God is Man, and exists in us and we in Him... The eternal body of Man is the imagination, that is, God Himself." -Neville Goddard

One of the most precious gifts God gave us, other than life itself, is the divine ability to imagine. Through imagination, God gave humanity the most sacred power, the ability to consciously shape, design, and transform the experience of life with out thoughts and imagination. This is not a small gift; it is the essence of our creative partnership with the Divine. The imagination is not child's play, it is spiritual power in motion. It is the language through which God speaks vision into being.

We are not powerless beings adrift in the chaos of circumstance. We are conscious creators, divine co-authors of our destiny, participants in an ever-unfolding masterpiece painted by the Eternal Source through us. Every thought, every feeling, every word is a brushstroke upon the canvas of creation.

Life does not simply happen *to* us, it happens *through* us, *as* us, and often *because* of us.

Even as a young woman, I can remember getting lost in daydreams, not realizing that my imagination was already shaping the world around me. I didn't yet understand that my thoughts were creative energy in motion, that I was just as capable of attracting struggle as I was of attracting joy. Back then, I drifted wherever my mind wandered. But now, I know better. I know that when my thoughts slip into fear or lack, I must gently bring them back to what I wish to see and feel. Because the truth is simple and powerful: **Thoughts create things.**

The moment we awaken to this truth, we step into our spiritual authority. Mind is all and it is no longer just a tool; it becomes a divine portal. The imagination, that sacred inner space where vision is born, becomes the meeting ground between human thought and divine will. Neville Goddard called it "the creative power of God within man." Everything we experience in the outer world is the reflection of what we have first held, believed, or imagined within.

When I first heard that truth, I wanted to believe it, but part of me wrestled with doubt. How could something invisible, our imagination, have the power to create something so tangible, so real? Yet when I looked back over my life, I saw the evidence everywhere. Every major breakthrough,every business I started, every book I wrote, every transformation, began first as a thought, a whisper, an inspired image that lived inside my heart before it ever took form in my hands. The inner always becomes the outer. What we nurture in consciousness must eventually express itself in the physical world. This is divine law.

Watch a child at play, and you will witness pure creative power in its most natural form. Children have not yet been taught to doubt their imagination. They build castles out of clouds and kingdoms from dust. They speak to invisible friends and create entire worlds that feel vividly real to them. They do not question whether they are "pretending," they simply *know* what they see in their mind's eye is real to their spirit.

I remember when my youngest daughter, **Journey Schy**, was only five years old. She once told me a story of standing on a rock deep underwater, feeling completely safe and serene. Another time, she said she was floating high above the ceiling, looking down at herself peacefully sleeping in bed. There was such innocence in her voice, and such certainty. She wasn't confused or afraid; she was connected.

This is what Jesus meant when He said, *"Unless you become as little children, you will not enter the kingdom of heaven."* The kingdom is not a faraway place among the clouds, it is a state of consciousness. It is the awareness that imagination and faith are the keys that unlock divine creation. Children live in that state naturally; adults must find their way back to it. As we grow older, we drift from this natural gift. We are taught to believe only in what can be seen, measured, or proven. The inner world becomes secondary, even dismissed as "unreal." But the truth is, the unseen is the birthplace of all that is seen. The thoughts we focus on in our mind become our objective reality. Every structure, invention, home, work of art, and healing began in someone's imagination. When we reclaim that sacred power, we reclaim our divine inheritance.

Like many people, I once believed that my imagination was something that happened to me, flashes of fantasy or daydreams I couldn't control. I didn't realize that I could choose, direct, or discipline my imagination. Now I know that imagination is a creative command. We have the ability to command our day from the moment we wake up.

There are still moments when a fearful image crosses my mind, a vision of something going wrong, or someone I love in danger. Or I may glimpse the morning news filled with crime, death, and destruction and carry it with me throughout the day. But now, instead of dwelling there, I shift. I change the scene. I breathe in light and create a new image, one of safety, joy, and divine order. I use my mouth to speak affirming words out loud. That simple act transforms my vibration immediately.

This is what I call *mind shifting.* You are not a passive observer of your inner world, you are its author. The thoughts you repeat and combine with emotion become scripts for the reality that plays out around you. When you "catch and cast," when you catch a negative thought and cast it out, you

125

reclaim your power. Like the *Recognize, Reject, and Replace* principle I taught earlier, this is the practice of divine mental alignment. You are practicing unshakable belief at the level of imagination.

Everything you have read in this book leads to one truth: **Mind Is All.** Not metaphorically or symbolically but practically. The universe operates like a mirror, vast, patient, and precise, but the mirror does not choose the image. The mind does. Life reflects not what we wish for, but what we consistently entertain, believe, and sustain within. The ideas we give authority to become the structure of our experience. The inner conversation becomes the outer condition.

This is why self-perception is one of the most powerful creative forces we possess. How you see yourself determines what ideas you allow to live in your mind. Those ideas, once accepted, quietly begin shaping your reality. When the mind accepts worth, life responds with opportunity. When the mind accepts limitation, life mirrors constraint. The reflection is neutral. The direction comes from within.

Throughout this book, we have explored one central principle: Everything begins with the mind. Ideas are energy and they instruct the nervous system, influence emotion, and guide behavior. When an idea is held long enough, it becomes belief. When belief is reinforced with emotion, it becomes expectation. And expectation is what the world eventually answers.

I often remind myself, *abundance is real*, because I understand that the mind must be led, especially in moments of uncertainty. When unexpected expenses arise or fear tries to take the wheel, the work is not to deny reality, but to **redirect the dominant idea**. Panic tightens the mind. Trust opens it. What you repeatedly imagine is not fantasy; it is rehearsal. The mind practices the future before the body ever experiences it.

Many teachers across time have named this same truth differently. Some call it faith. Some call it the law of attraction. Some call it alignment. But beneath every label is the same mechanism: **energy responds to thought because thought leads energy**. As Wayne Dyer said, *you'll see it when you believe it*. Belief is not hoping, it is mental acceptance. And acceptance is instruction.

As this understanding deepened for me, my focus shifted away from proving anything to the world and toward something far more important: **legacy**. Knowing that life is temporary makes the responsibility of thought more sacred. I want my children, and anyone who reads these words, to understand that imagination is not escape. It is direction for the mind. Life is like a coloring book, and only you hold the crayons. What you color repeatedly becomes the picture you live inside of. Only you have the crayons to design the life you desire.

This awareness was tested during a quiet but pivotal moment in my life. In early 2025, during a slow season in my business, I was preparing for a major transition, selling my home of twenty-six years and relocating my family. The excitement was real, but so was the pressure. When I realized the cost of moving alone exceeded eleven thousand dollars and income had slowed significantly, the moment demanded a choice: allow fear to dominate the mind, or consciously choose a higher idea. I chose intention.

Each day, I returned my thoughts to gratitude and trust, not because fear wasn't present, but because fear did not deserve to consume me. One afternoon, while working quietly, a calm knowing settled in. Not hope. Not wishful thinking, but knowing. Within minutes, a client I hadn't heard from in over a year reached out, booked an appointment, and sent a large deposit. That moment was not coincidence. It was confirmation that the mind had aligned, and life had responded.

This is the responsibility that comes with understanding that **Mind Is All**. Creation is not random. It is feedback. Every experience, pleasant or painful, is information about the ideas we have been sustaining. When we become conscious of this, life stops feeling chaotic and starts feeling instructive.

I learned this lesson deeply through grief as well. For years, I replayed the traumatic loss of my grandmother over and over in my mind, unknowingly keeping myself bound to pain. Each replay reinforced the wound. Healing began when I changed the image. I chose to remember her life instead of her death. The moment I redirected the story, peace followed. Healing does not require forgetting, it requires **re-framing**. The mind must be guided toward what heals, not what harms.

This is what it means to live as a conscious creator. Not perfection, but true awareness. Awareness of the stories we tell ourselves and the images we replay in our minds. Awareness of which ideas we allow to lead. When awareness is present, choice returns and where choice exists, creation becomes intentional. You always have a choice to reset your thinking pattern and steer your mind in the direction of happiness, great health, peace, love and prosperity.

You are not a victim of circumstance. You are the master of your fate. A living extension of divine imagination. When you change the way you think, the world must respond differently. Your thoughts are powerful and they create your reality. With this power comes responsibility. You cannot dwell in fear and expect peace to flourish. You cannot nurture resentment and anger expect love to flow. Every thought is a seed in the garden of your mind. Every emotion is the water. The life you experience is the harvest.

To live by the truth that **Mind Is All** is to tend to your inner world with reverence. To choose thoughts that heal and make you feel good and release thoughts and ideas that limit you. Learning to monitor your thoughts is the ultimate power. This is the key to creating a life free of limitations for yourself.

Every word you speak is a direction. The images you chose to focus on mentally are the instructions. When imagination aligns with belief, manifestation follows.

✦ Final Affirmation:
I understand that Mind Is All.
I choose my thoughts with intention, my emotions with awareness,
and my focus with purpose.
I direct my inner world wisely, knowing that My mind shapes my reality.

MIND = M - Manipulate I - Ideas in a N - New D - Direction

About the Author

~~~~~~~~~~~~~

SaBrina Fisher Reece was once known throughout California as *"The Braid Queen."*

For over twenty-six years, she owned and operated the legendary **Braids By SaBrina**, a celebrated salon and school on Adams Boulevard in Los Angeles. It became the largest and most influential braiding establishment in the city, a place where artistry, empowerment, and community beautifully intertwined.

As SaBrina stepped into the second half of her life, she felt a divine calling to share the deeper story behind her success, a journey of faith, transformation, and inner peace. What began as a career of creativity evolved into a life of purpose. She now inspires others through her writing and motivational speaking, guiding people toward healing and self-discovery.

She is the author of *My Spiritual Smile*, **Unbroken**, *How Do I Control My Emotions?*, *Kicking Depression In the Butt*, *Self-Sabotage*, and *Perfectly Positive, Living life on a Higher Frequency*, *The BALANCE & FOCUS 2 book Series, and many more*, each one a reflection of her own awakening.

SaBrina is a devoted mother of four, **Justin, Joi, Jayden, and Journey,** and a proud grandmother to **Raiden Jesse** and **Rio Jordan**. Her greatest joy is watching them, and all those she teaches, awaken to their divine potential.

Her passion for sound and frequency has led her to explore the healing power of **crystal sound bowls, tuning forks, and flow chimes,** tools that help harmonize the body, mind, and spirit. Yet, she reminds her students and readers that there is no single path to peace. Every person's journey is sacred, and every method of connecting with the Divine is worthy.

Now residing in the enchanting landscapes of **New Mexico, "The Land of Enchantment,"** SaBrina offers **Sound Vibration Sessions** that invite others to slow down, breathe deeply, and reconnect with their higher selves.

Her message is simple, timeless, and true:

"We were each born with divine energy, a God-given power to create, to heal, and to live a full happy life. The goal is not perfection, but peace.

The journey is not to escape life, but to embrace it. To Utilize positive tools to take control of your mindset and become the Master of your fate.

You can connect with me on:
- https://in59secondspublishing.com
- https://www.facebook.com/BraidQueenSaBrinaReece

Also by SaBrina Fisher Reece

SaBrina Fisher Reece is an author, entrepreneur, and metaphysical teacher whose work centers on the power of thought, focus, and conscious awareness. Through her writing, she explores how the mind influences emotional well-being, personal growth, and the direction of one's life. Her books blend practical insight with spiritual principles, offering readers grounded tools for strengthening mental discipline and cultivating intentional thinking.

With a background in entrepreneurship and decades of real-world experience, SaBrina brings a relatable and honest voice to the self-help and metaphysical space. Her work emphasizes personal responsibility, focus, and the ability to consciously redirect thoughts and energy toward more constructive outcomes. Rather than promoting idealism or perfection, she encourages awareness, consistency, and self-mastery as pathways to change.

SaBrina Fisher Reece is the author of multiple self-help titles focused on mindset, focus, emotional awareness, and inner balance. Her writing speaks to readers seeking clarity, stability, and a deeper understanding of how their inner world shapes their outer experience.

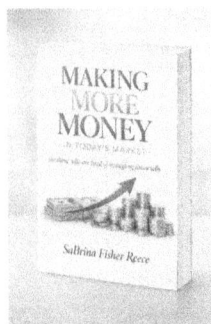

Making More Money in Today's Market
Making More Money in Today's Market
For Those Who Are Tired of Struggling Financially
By SaBrina Fisher Reece

If you are tired of working hard but feeling stuck, tired of doing "everything right" yet still worrying about money, or tired of believing that financial freedom is for other people, this book was written for you.

Making more money is not just about strategy. It's about mindset, focus, and expectation. Long before income changes, belief has to shift. This book begins there.

SaBrina Fisher Reece shares her honest perspective on money, success, and prosperity, not from a place of theory, but from lived experience. She has always expected money to flow, and that expectation shaped her decisions, her confidence, and her results. She also understands that many people were never taught to think that way. They were taught to survive, to settle, or to fear financial growth.

This book is not about shaming where you started. It is about showing you how to change your relationship with money so you can experience more ease, stability, and abundance in this lifetime.

Inside these pages, you will learn how to:

Shift the beliefs that quietly limit your income

Understand money as an exchange of value, not struggle

Develop focus in a market full of distraction

Build confidence around earning, charging, and receiving

Stop repeating financial patterns that no longer serve you

Create a mindset that supports growth in today's economy

This is not a get-rich-quick promise. It is a practical, empowering guide to thinking differently about money so your actions can finally produce different results. Whether you want to increase your income, start a business, grow an existing one, or simply feel less stressed about finances, this book meets you where you are and shows you what's possible next.

You do not need permission to want more.

You do not need to struggle forever.

You can learn to expect better.

Making More Money in Today's Market is an invitation to shift your focus, expand your expectations, and step into a more prosperous future, starting now.

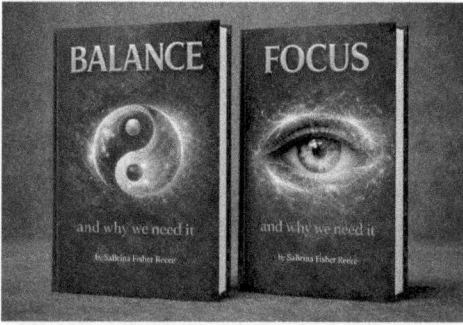

The Balance & Focus 2 Book Series

The Balance & Focus Series is designed to help readers return to themselves in a world that constantly pulls them off center. These books explore two essential elements of a grounded, intentional life: inner balance and conscious focus.

Balance examines how alignment between mind, body, and energy creates stability, emotional clarity, and resilience, even during life's most challenging moments. *Focus* builds on that foundation by exploring the power of attention, intention, and mental discipline, showing how clarity and direction shape the outcomes we experience.

Together, these books offer practical insight and spiritual awareness for those seeking to live with greater purpose, presence, and self-mastery. This series is not about perfection, but about learning how to steady yourself, direct your energy wisely, and create a life that feels aligned from the inside out.

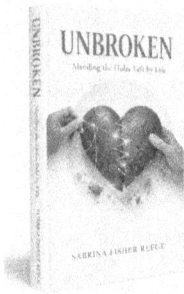

Unbroken

Unbroken: Mending the Holes Left by Life is a deeply honest exploration of healing after trauma, loss, abandonment, and emotional pain. This book is for anyone who has survived experiences that left invisible wounds and wondered if wholeness was ever possible again.

Through personal reflection, spiritual insight, and emotional awareness, SaBrina Fisher Reece examines how unresolved pain creates "holes" in the heart and mind, shaping our thoughts, reactions, relationships, and sense of self. Rather than approaching healing through blame or denial, *Unbroken* invites readers to understand their wounds with compassion and learn how to begin mending them from the inside out.

This book explores themes of emotional balance, self-awareness, forgiveness, spiritual grounding, and the power of the mind to either trap us in the past or guide us toward freedom. SaBrina shares her journey of survival, growth, and transformation, illustrating how it is possible to build a meaningful life even while carrying pain, and how healing does not require perfection, only honesty.

Unbroken is not about pretending life did not hurt. It is about learning how to live fully without allowing past trauma to control the present. It is a guide for those ready to stop surviving and start healing, reclaim their inner strength, and reconnect with the love that has always existed beneath the pain.

If you have ever felt fragmented, overwhelmed, or defined by what you endured, this book will remind you of a powerful truth. You are not broken. You are becoming.

Spiritual Balance

Spiritual Balance: Aligning Mind, Body, and Energy in Everyday Life is a grounded, insightful guide for anyone seeking clarity, emotional stability, and deeper alignment in a fast-moving world.

In this book, SaBrina Fisher Reece explores the truth that many people sense but struggle to articulate: life becomes chaotic when our inner energies are out of balance. Drawing from spiritual principles, lived experience, and practical awareness, *Spiritual Balance* breaks down how the mind, body, and energetic self are deeply interconnected, and how neglecting one inevitably affects the others.

This book reframes common spiritual concepts in a way that is accessible, realistic, and applicable to everyday life. Readers will learn that masculine and feminine energies are not tied to gender, but are universal forces present within every person. When these energies are balanced, we experience greater peace, confidence, emotional regulation, and healthier relationships. When they are not, stress, confusion, and emotional exhaustion take over.

Rather than offering abstract philosophy, *Spiritual Balance* provides readers with a new way of understanding themselves. It encourages self-awareness, intentional living, and emotional responsibility without shame or perfectionism. Topics include emotional balance, energetic boundaries, spiritual awareness, self-worth, and the role of unseen forces in shaping our daily experiences.

This book is for readers who know there is more to life than what can be seen, measured, or explained logically, but who also want something practical, grounded, and honest. *Spiritual Balance* meets spirituality where real life happens: in relationships, work, healing, growth, and everyday decisions.

By aligning mind, body, and energy, readers are guided toward a more peaceful, empowered, and intentional way of living, one that honors both the human experience and the spiritual truth beneath it.

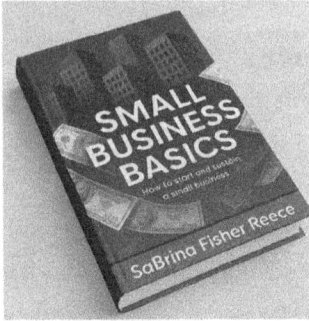

Small Business Basics

Small Business Basics is the powerful story of how a young woman with no blueprint, no support, and no safety net built one of Los Angeles' most recognized braid studios, and the step-by-step guide she created so others could rise too.

Through raw honesty and decades of wisdom, SaBrina Fisher Reece reveals the lessons that shaped her journey: how to start before you're ready, how to visualize success, how to market with courage, how to lead with compassion, how to set boundaries, and how to build a business that reflects your purpose, not your past.

This book blends practical business strategies with personal growth, healing, and spiritual insight, reminding readers that entrepreneurship is not just about making money, it's about becoming the strongest version of yourself. If you're ready to build a business rooted in discipline, faith, confidence, and heart, this book will show you the way.

www.ingramcontent.com/pod-product-compliance
Lightning Source LLC
LaVergne TN
LVHW011203080426
835508LV00007B/577